Prayer Strategies for Breaking the Curse of Genocide Against the Jews

Calling Christians to Stand with the Jewish People

Zeb Bradford Long

With Discernment, Reflections and Prayers

Martin Boardman

PRMI

EXOUSIA PRESS

Prayer Strategies for Breaking the Curse of Genocide Against the Jews—Calling Christians to Stand with the Jewish People
Copyright © 2024 Zeb Bradford Long

All rights reserved; however, any part of this book that may aid in discernment and prayer to advance the Gospel of Jesus Christ may be reproduced without seeking permission or acknowledging the author.

Published by PRMI Exousia Press, a ministry of the Presbyterian-Reformed Ministries International Dunamis Institute

Black Mountain, North Carolina, USA
www.prmi.org

Cover design and graphics by Stephanie Ferguson

Cover illustration: Public domain. Warsaw Ghetto Uprising (Poland) – Photo from Jürgen Stroop Report to Heinrich Himmler from May 1943. One of the most famous pictures of World War II. The Jews— men women and children, forced out of the Ghetto were shipped to Treblinka and to other extermination centers.

Scripture quoted by permission. Unless otherwise indicated, all scripture quotations are taken from the NET Bible® copyright ©1996-2016 by Biblical Studies Press, L.L.C. All rights reserved.

Because of the dynamic nature of the Internet, any web addresses or links contained in this book may have changed since publication and may no longer be valid.

ISBN: 978-1-7339269-6-6

"Silence in the face of evil is itself evil: God will not hold us guiltless. Not to speak is to speak. Not to act is to act."

— Attributed to Dietrich Bonhoeffer

WRITE THIS FOR A REMEMRANCE IN A BOOK…THAT THE LORD HAS A WAR WITH AMALEK FROM GENERATION TO GENERATION.

Exodus 17

From the title page of the book *War and Remembrance* – By Herman Wouk

But what God foretold through the mouth of all His prophets—that His Messiah was to suffer—so He has fulfilled. Repent, therefore, and return—so your sins might be blotted out, so times of relief [refreshing] might come from the presence of Adonai, and He might send Yeshua [Jesus], the Messiah appointed for you. Heaven must receive Him, until the time of the restoration of all the things that God spoke about long ago through the mouth of His holy prophets.

Acts 3:18-21 TLV

ACKNOWLEDGMENTS

I am deeply grateful for the many people who have made this book possible. First, my gratitude to Stephanie Ferguson for her work as editor, designing the cover, creating charts, and expert formatting. My thanks also go to Lonnie Shields, who has a Pentecostal background and who is an excellent editor, helping to find things we often missed and keeping us rooted in the Bible and awake to the Holy Spirit.

Especially important to me has been the input from Messianic Jewish leaders, some located in Israel and some in the United States. Their keen wisdom and insights from the Jewish perspective have deepened my own biblical worldview, in which God's redemptive plans revolve around Jerusalem and the Jewish people and then all the rest of us who are engrafted in through Jesus Christ. I especially want to thank Grant and Hali Berry of Reconnecting Ministries for their personal friendship and passion for connecting born-again Jews and Gentiles together as the One New Man, which is essential for reversing this curse and for preparing the way for the Next Great Awakening.

Special thanks to Steve Aceto who helps me constantly keep my eyes on Jesus Christ, the one who, in himself on the Cross, reverses all curses with blessings!

Most critical for this process is my "War Room" and the Mountain Top Equipping Camps that have taken place at the Community of the Cross in North Carolina. This team has joined with me for years in the frontline engagements in strategic level intercession and spiritual warfare. This is the context in which this discernment of Satan's plans, as well as our calling to cooperate with the Holy Spirit in advancing the Kingdom of God over them, has taken place. It provides the basis of the prophetic declarations as well as prayer tactics recommended in this book.

Thanks also for the Executive International Leadership Team of PRMI for their support for me in this project. Especially for Rev. Cindy Strickler, Director of PRMI whose role in shared leadership in PRMI, as well as her practical advice, has been invaluable in implementing such inherently dangerous and potentially disruptive actions of publicly naming and, with the Holy Spirit, reversing this curse of genocide against the Jewish people that has been unleashed after the October 7th Massacre of Jews. She has helped to keep me on track with the overall mission of PRMI even while following Jesus in radical obedience in this project which is so urgent that it could tilt the whole ministry away from God's central purposes. In addition, I thank Martin Boardman, Director of Prayer Mobilization, for his chapter summaries and prayer points. And I thank Paul Stokes, Director of the Dunamis Institute and of the Dunamis Fellowship in Britian and Ireland, for major review and editing.

I must also thank the PRMI Board for providing support for the book as both prayer guidance as well as a prophetic declaration, to be printed and distributed under the PRMI Exousia Press. In doing so it puts this ministry on record that we are not being silent, as many Christians were during the 1930s, which was the last time that Jew-hatred and calls for the extermination of the Jewish people went viral.

I also must thank Laura, my wife of 49 years, who has been immensely supportive of and shared in the toll of the intensive prayer engagements as well as the intensity of writing.

Thanks to everyone who has made getting this book out possible including those who prayed for me and the ministry. I hope and pray, that it is in God's time, to take part in His plans to reverse the curse of genocide of the Jews before the tipping point is reached and we descend into the abyss of a second holocaust and a third global war.

Table of Contents

ACKNOWLEDGMENTS 5

Prologue 9

1 - The October 7th Hamas Massacre of Jews 19

2 - Five Biblical Principles for Understanding the Hamas Massacre of October 7th, 2023 25

3 - Exposing Two Expressions of the Antichrist Spirit: Islam and Marxism 33

4 - Extermination of the Jewish People—Really? 41

5 - God's Master Plans for His Kingdom to Come 53

6 - Why Now, in the 2020s, Is Jew-hatred on the Rise? 63

7 - Exposing Satan's Use of Curses to Dethrone God 73

8 - God's War Against Amalek 89

9 - Announcing: God is at War with Hamas and Others Cursing Israel 117

10 - Breaking the Curses of Genocide 127

11 - As One New Humanity, Preparing for a Great Outpouring of the Holy Spirit 151

Postscript: Engaging High-Level Demonic Powers 157

Prologue

In this second decade of the twenty-first century, we are at an unprecedented tipping point in reaching Jesus Christ's conditions for His return in glory: the Jewish people returning to the Land of Israel and to saving faith in Yeshua Ha Mashiach (Jesus the Messiah) and the Gospel of the Kingdom being preached to all nations. The fulfillment of God the Father's redemptive plans is being driven forward by outpourings of the Holy Spirit, igniting revivals worldwide. In the vanguard of these revival movements are Holy Spirit empowered born-again Jews who remain Jews, and Holy Spirit empowered born-again non-Jews who also keep their identity but are joined in unity in Jesus/Yeshua, as the "One New Man" of Ephesians chapter 2. We are indeed at an amazing time in the history of the world!

Satan's Plans for Genocide of the Jews to Block God's Redemptive Plans

Parallel to this global move of the Holy Spirit, there are ominous stirrings of Satan working to counter and quench this great revival. The nature of this counterattack against God's Kingdom has been both exposed and catalyzed in the October 7th, 2023, Hamas Massacre of Jews. This abhorrent event has revealed that at the heart of Satan's plans is the destruction of Israel and the genocide of the Jewish people. This event unmasks the reality that in this decade of the 2020s, we are facing the unthinkable – a call for the extermination of Jews and Christians, and indeed, a large portion of humanity! It is a call coming from diverse, discordant movements: radical Islamist, Marxist, the anti-humanist extreme strand of environmentalism,[1] and others, whose unifying characteristic is their schemes to impose their 'solution' on the world will result in genocide.

The October 7th massacre is only one event, among others. But it is significant because history teaches us that when hatred erupts against the Jews, it starts a contagion of evil that spreads well beyond them. I will be showing in this book that Satan is working primarily in our present epoch through an unholy alliance of strongholds based on the antichrist ideologies of Islam and Marxism. Through these Satan is launching a campaign first of Jew-hatred, which creates the conditions for fulfilling the curse of genocide, which is in order to block this outpouring Holy Spirit that is fulfilling the Great Commission. Deeper and more terrible than subverting the impending great revival is Satan's plan to dethrone God's rule and presence on earth by exterminating first Jews and then those who have been grafted into them through faith in Jesus Christ.

We must not underestimate the severity of the present situation. The plans of Satan and his deceived agents are so horrific, so evil and inhuman that we are tempted to dismiss them as improbable and impossible. Yet therein lies the danger. A century ago, the world dismissed the warnings about Adolf Hitler's hate-filled genocidal intent towards Jews and Slavic people, seemingly oblivious to the hellish visions that were encapsulated in his writings and policies. Seeds of genocide in Marxism were also exposed when Joseph Stalin and Mao Zedong implemented their

---

[1] This does not include everyone who has concerns for the environment which would include myself! Rather I am speaking of the anti-humanity extremes of this movement. This extreme is represented in the now destroyed "Georgia Guidestones." The first guideline is "Maintain humanity under 500,000,000 in perpetual balance with nature." The 10th is "Be not a cancer on the earth—Leave room for nature—Leave room for nature." The implications of their dictates would include the extermination of a large portion of humanity. https://jashow.org/articles/the-new-ten-commandments-the-georgia-guidestones/

utopian visions through campaigns of persecution, execution, and starvation that far surpassed Hitler's death tally. Their targets were Christians and other entire classes of people who did not fit the vision of the Workers' Paradise. Through the 1930s and into the 1950s, even up to the present, blindness to the evils and the fruit of Islamism, Nazism, and Marxism/Leninism resulted in a global catastrophe with millions of dead, entire nations in ruins, and incalculable human misery and suffering.

These expressions of demonic evil had their roots in many things, including the rise of the occult and the deception of antichrist ideologies. But above all there was the rise of antisemitism. Hatred of Jews and attacks against the Jews are the harbingers and forewarnings of the increase of demonic evil in society and the precursor to genocide, starting with the Jews but rarely ending with them.

The Clarion Call to Intercessors as the First Step for Breaking Satan's Plans for Genocide

We dare not be blind this time; otherwise, this disaster will be even worse than it was a century ago. In those days, the Lord raised up anointed prophets such as Pastor Bonhoeffer, who warned of the dangers and called the Church to oppose the impending evil in word and deed. God called Rees Howells, in Great Britain, to mobilize an army of intercessors who travailed and prevailed in prayer to expose and thwart the onslaught of unimaginable evil. The Lord also raised up courageous statesmen such as Winston Churchill, who named the danger and, in the 12th hour, was finally in a leadership role to oppose it. Similarly in our day, the Lord is speaking through His prophets naming the evil. He is calling forth a fresh army of intercessors who must rise up and play their part. Alongside this spiritual dimension, the Lord is also raising up political and military leaders through whom He will wage war against all who are seeking the destruction of the Jewish people and of those engrafted into them through Jesus Christ.

In this book, we are naming the evil of Jew-hatred and unflinchingly declaring that, if unchecked in the human and spiritual realms, it leads to the fulfillment of the curse of genocide. As in the epoch of the 1930s to the 40s, the conditions are being put in place for this to ignite a global disaster that may be a second Holocaust of those of biblical faith and World War III, with a potential death toll of billions.

We believe that the roots of this madness into which the world seems to be descending are, ultimately, coming from Satan, who is instigating Jew-hatred and empowering the curse of genocide, and provoking the nations to war. The purpose is to prevent the revival that is already underway. This is a revival that may well become the End Times Great Awakening, in which the Gospel of the Kingdom is preached to all nations and all of Israel is saved through faith in Yeshua the Messiah.

So, against this cacophony of evil and the winds of war, which seem to be gaining gale force, this book is written to call the church into action. We are called to the following: exposing the evils, naming and breaking the curse of genocide, praying for those who are on the frontlines of the Lord's battle, and, above all, praying for God's redemptive plans to be fulfilled.

Intercession is the Vanguard of Advancing the Kingdom of God on Earth

Our Lord Jesus Christ tells us to pray: "Your kingdom come, Your will be done on earth as it is in heaven…" (Mat 6:10 TLV) Praying for God's kingdom includes prophetically naming the evils blocking the Kingdom so that they may be removed and praying for the outpouring of the Holy Spirit which will enable the advance of the Gospel of Jesus Christ.

This is modeled for us in Acts 4:23-31. This is right after the first outpouring of the Holy Spirit at Pentecost, when Satan is opposing the advancement of the Gospel. The disciples pray, "Lord, look at their threats." They name these threats: those attacking Jesus' earthly expression of the move of God. "For truly both Herod and

Pontius Pilate, along with the Gentiles and the peoples of Israel, were gathered together in this city against Your holy Servant Yeshua, whom You anointed." (Acts 4:27 TLV) In this book, we are doing just this: boldy exposing and naming these present threats and prophetically announcing that God is at war against them, and He is calling us to join in His war. As I am called to address the church in this book, the focus will be on our primary calling, which will be on prophetically naming the evil, breaking the curses, and praying for the outpouring of the Holy Spirit. We will also show that this work includes praying for those through whom God is working to defeat this evil, which includes intercession for those called into God's war. This includes the opinion makers, the governments and military leaders of the nations, and those on the frontlines of the conflict.

So, in addition to prophetically exposing this curse of genocide and identifying those through whom Satan is working, the vanguard is the work of intercessory prayer and spiritual warfare. This book is an urgent call issued to those whom the Lord has anointed as intercessors, spiritual warriors who are called to expose Satan's plans and participate with God the Father, Son, and Holy Spirit in defeating them.

Why This Work of Intercession Must Now Go Public

Usually, this work of intercession remains hidden and restricted to a few well-trained and highly anointed intercessors. A small team of PRMI intercessors, which is just one small tributary in a great river of prayer, have been called into this strategic-level intercession and spiritual warfare. We will continue to be about this work of intercession. However, after the October 7th, 2023, Hamas massacre of the Jews, I have been given clear guidance that the Lord is calling me to publish this book intended for a wider audience well beyond the limits of our teams of anointed and well-equipped intercessors. The rationale for going public is as follows: October 7th marked a shift that has taken place in Satan's tactics and now the Lord is calling us to alter our tactics accordingly.

The October 7ᵗʰ Massacre indicates that Satan is moving his attack plans against the Jewish people and God's Kingdom from covert and largely hidden work to overt attacks. These overt attacks revealed his true purposes, which are the destruction of Israel and the extermination of the Jewish people. The Hamas Massacre of Jews was a globally publicized event and catalyzed global movements of Jew-hatred, the antichrist ideologies behind it, and it disseminated the curse of genocide of the Jews worldwide. This is creating the demonic, cultural, political, and geopolitical conditions conducive to the destruction of Israel and the genocide of the Jews.

I believe that to counter and defeat these plans of Satan, the Lord God is calling us to expose these plans of Satan now publicly and to announce His intentions of defeating the curse of genocide spoken and acted against the Jewish people. So, this requires that this document exposes these dangers and gives the prayer strategies that we are called to deploy to go further out into the public domain. This going public in book form is not just for opening human eyes to the dangers but will serve as a notice in the spiritual realm to the powers and principalities behind this evil.

Our prayer is that the Holy Spirit will use this book to break these curses of genocide, defeat these demonic strongholds, and open wide the doors for the continued outpouring of the Holy Spirit, leading to the fulfillment of the biblical promise of the restorations of all things. (Acts 3:18-21)

The battle is taking place in real-time!

Remember that this book is not being written in retrospect but in the middle of a crisis. We are in the midst of a constantly evolving and escalating conflict. The outcome at this point in at the completion of writing this book in March of 2024 is very much in doubt. I am rushing the publication of this book to prepare intercessors, in cooperation with the Holy Spirit, to prevent the worst-case scenarios from happening as they did the last time the world suffered a pandemic of Jew-hatred.

The descriptions of the battle strategies and tactics that the Holy Spirit calls us to deploy are backed up with only a minimum of present examples, and with little proof of their validity. However, what I am offering is based on in-depth Bible study, a study of history, and extensive experience in strategic-level intercession. What I present here draws from my other books based on previous prayer battles, and in those I give a fuller explanation of these prayer strategies. Of particular relevance to this present battle with Hamas and other Islamic groups threatening genocide of the Jews are my books dealing with previous battles defeating expressions of Radical Islam, Al Qaeda, Iran, the War in Iraq, and the Islamic State. In those books, you can see the confirmation of how God worked through these strategies.[2]

The Call for Christians to Stand with the Jewish People

This book is also an urgent call for the Church of Jesus Christ – for all Christians worldwide – to NOT do what most of us did in the 1930s when Jew-hatred was on the rise and Satan was gathering the means to fulfill the curse of genocide against the Jewish people. In that time of gathering demonic evil, with a few notable exceptions, the church in Germany, the UK and USA were blind to the evil and remained silent. During that period before the Nazis exerted totalitarian control there was a window of opportunity when the German Church could have stood with the Jews but did not. This was especially so from 1933 to 1935 when the "Ayryan Clause" was enforced, removing born again Jews from the clergy. This approach was opposed by Pastor Bonhoeffer and the "confessing church" but not by the whole National German Church which had major cultural influence at the time. There was also a window of opportunity when the world Church, especially in England and the USA, could have stood with the Jews and spoken against the Jew-hatred and persecution of them by the Nazis.

---

[2] See my books *Discerning the Times* and *Prayer Strategy for Jesus' Victory*.

Again, a few did so, such as Rees Howells, but for the most part there was silence or, worse still, agreement with the antisemitism of that era. As a result, the Church of Jesus Christ was often complicit in the fulfillment of the curse of genocide — the Holocaust.[3]

I am convinced that right now we are in a similar window of opportunity, in which Christians can make a decisive difference in blocking the fulfillment of the curse of genocide against the Jewish people, by standing with them through intercession, prophetic declarations and decisive supportive actions.

The intercessors and spiritual warriors are the vanguard in opposing Satan and advancing the Kingdom of God. But we are only one small part of the body of Christ. Behind us must be the rest of the Church. This is a call for intercessors to arise, follow Jesus Christ as our commander and Savior, and join the battle! I believe with all my heart that if we act now in response to what Jesus has revealed to us and follow His guidance then, instead of a disaster that could be Holocaust 2.0 and World War III, the Jewish people will continue to flourish in the Land of Israel and will come to saving faith in the Yeshua the Messiah, and that the gospel of the Kingdom will go to all nations.

God – Father, Son, and Holy Spirit, is calling us into intercession and to cooperate with Him in exposing and defeating Satan's plans for genocide. The purpose in calling us to join Him in this war is to fulfill His Word spoken through Jeremiah (Jeremiah 3:16-18) and Paul (Romans 11:11-15) to the Jewish people and the Church of Jesus Christ so that the great revival that has already begun will not be blocked but will thrive, will continue to go global and will become the Next Great Awakening, ushering in the End Times and the "restoration of all things through, "Yeshua the Messiah." (Acts 3:21) If we Christians fail to stand with the Jewish people this time then the results will be the reign of unfathomable evil.

---

[3] This history is confined and extensively documented in Eric Matrix's two books, *Bonhoeffer: Pastor, Martyr, Prophet, Spy* and, *Letter to the American Church*.

Breaking the Curse of Genocide against the Jews

1

The October 7th Hamas Massacre of Jews

On October 7th, 2023, Hamas, the terrorist organization that controls Gaza, launched a massive, coordinated attack over land, sea, and air—with over 2,200 rockets shot into Israel within a 20-minute window[4]. Under cover of aerial bombardment, some 3,000 Islamic jihadists broke through the security barriers, entered many Israeli villages and kibbutzim, and murdered over 1,300 men, women, and children. The number of victims continues to grow as more bodies are found. This is the worst atrocity against the Jews since the Holocaust during the Nazi reign of barbarism in the 1930s and 1940s.

Jihadists gunned down entire groups of innocent people, beheaded children and babies, gang-raped women and children while forcing others to watch, mutilated men and women, and burned alive whole families in their homes. Children and families were tortured to death. Several hundred men, women, and

---

[4] https://abcnews.go.com/International/timeline-surprise-rocket-attack-hamas-israel/story?id=103816006

Chapter 1 The October 7th Hamas Massacre of the Jews

children were kidnapped and taken back to Gaza.

The murderers filmed these atrocities and posted the carnage on the internet, sometimes on the victims' own phones and social media accounts. Against the background screams of their victims, the Islamists are seen gleefully rejoicing and shouting, "Allahu Akbar" ("Allah is Greater!"). The BBC[5] reported accounts of body parts sliced off and tossed around like playthings, of a pregnant woman whose womb had been ripped open and her fetus stabbed while it was inside her before she was killed, and of hundreds of women who were stripped, mutilated, and then murdered. One gruesome and disturbing picture showed a near-naked, bloodied woman, perhaps still alive, tied to the front of a car being paraded through the streets of Gaza with its citizens cheering. These are nauseating images of horror, pure hatred, and evil.

See the image of just one woman who has been raped, and then

---

[5] Israel Gaza: Hamas raped and mutilated women on 7 October, BBC hears 5 December 2023. By Lucy Williamson Middle East correspondent, Jerusalem WARNING: CONTAINS EXTREMELY GRAPHIC DESCRIPTIONS OF SEXUAL VIOLENCE AND RAPE https://www.bbc.com/news/world-middle-east-67629181
1

abducted and taken back to Gaza. Many others were shown in the media, taken by the Jihadists themselves to show the entire world their gruesome deeds.

As news of these attacks spread around the world, and as Israel prepared and then began its response, a second attack began. This was not with guns and missiles, but a propaganda attack of words, images, and memes that elevated a pro-Hamas, anti-Israel and anti-Jewish narrative in the public consciousness. On the streets of London, Madrid, Athens, Amsterdam, Sydney, Hyderabad, Ottawa, Washington, and New York – and in many other cities around the world – crowds gathered to demonstrate public solidarity with Hamas and stir up anti-Jewish sentiment.[6]

The BLM (Black Lives Matter) chapter in Chicago posted a graphic on social media portraying a paraglider terror attack and proclaiming support for it. The slogan "From the River to the Sea" became a powerful piece of propaganda, popularizing a phrase that, fundamentally, requires the eradication of Israel as a nation.

If you look closely at the protesters, they are chanting "gas the Jews," calling for Holocaust 2.0 to complete the work of Hitler, and "from the river to the sea" - calling for the eradication of Israel as a nation. This rise of demonically energized and politically manipulated antisemitism is taking place not only on the streets of major Western cities, but also on the elite college campuses of the United States and the United Kingdom.

Much of this anti-Israel and antisemitic rhetoric and vocal support for Hamas began while the stunned citizens of Israel were

---

[6] https://en.wikipedia.org/wiki/2023_Israel%E2%80%93Hamas_war_protests

still locating their dead and having firefights with the Islamic jihadist terrorists in the country. Condemnation of Israel started before Israel's counterattacks had even begun.

This war, waged with words, has served to minimize compassion for the innocent Jews who were killed, raped, tortured, or dragged as captives back to Gaza. Instead, it has been stirring up renewed hatred of Jews and has the potential to escalate the outbreaks of evil worldwide. News outlets around the world reported arson and assaults on Jewish property and people, as well as a handful of alleged similar retaliatory attacks on Muslims.

Summary: Pointers for Praying

This is primarily a spiritual battle. Yes, we see and are influenced by events that take place in the physical realm. Military and political agendas are involved. But as the Apostle Paul reminds us:

> "Our struggle is not against flesh and blood, but against the rulers, against the authorities, against the powers of this dark world and against the spiritual forces of evil in the heavenly realms." (Ephesians 6:12 NIV)

As we engage in the work of prayer, we must remember that there are spiritual forces of good and evil that lie behind the physical realities of what is taking place. The work of intercession, directed always by the Holy Spirit, is to expose the work of the demonic, to pray that the plans of Satan are blocked and frustrated, and to pray that the plans of God are fulfilled.

The battle is spiritual, but it involves people and, sometimes, bloody military campaigns. We must hold fast to the truth that God loves everyone. He loves both the Jews and the Palestinians. Both are made in his image, and the Lord has plans and purposes for both. God is grieved by the effects of this war. He was present amid the massacre on October 7, and He wept both for the Jews who were being tortured and killed and for the Palestinians who were inflicting violence and hate. He weeps also for those who continue to die in the ongoing fighting.

God calls us to operate out of love and to seek His mercy, grace, and justice. So, as we pray, we need to do so with hearts aligned with God's heart. When Joshua encountered the commander of the army of the Lord as he was preparing to fight against Jericho, he asked him which side he was on. The commander's answer was "Neither" (Joshua 5:14). He was on the Lord's side! In the same way, we need to be on the Lord's side as we pray.

Therefore, as we pray:

- We must ask the Lord to shine His light into our hearts and expose our wrong motivations or attitudes.

- We must ask the Lord to fill us with His love and help us pray according to His will.

- We need to pray for the empowerment of the Holy Spirit and surrender ourselves to following the Spirit's lead.

- We need to pray for protection since this is a spiritual battle and ensure that we are wearing the armor of God and operating out of His love.

- We need to pray that the Holy Spirit will show us anything the enemy could use against us and allow the Spirit to lead us into confession and repentance.

Chapter 1 The October 7th Hamas Massacre of the Jews

2

Five Biblical Principles for Understanding the Hamas Massacre of October 7th, 2023.

Many are seeking to understand the October 7th Hamas Massacre of Jews and the events that are taking place in Israel, Gaza, and the broader Middle East. People are glued to media reports and trying to understand what is happening. Different groups have interpreted the events differently, and Christian believers are struggling to gain God's perspective and to know how to pray.[7]

This *Discerning the Times* aims to articulate what we believe is God's perspective on the events of October 7 (as we understand them) and the events that have continued to unfold and which, even now, seem to threaten to bring us all into a broader world war. Believers need to see the events from God's perspective so that they can pray and intercede and answer objections that they

---

[7] This chapter was originally published in *Discerning the Times*. https://discernwith.us/insights-and-prayers-navigating-recent-events-in-israel-gaza-and-the-middle-east

Chapter 2 Five Biblical Principles for Understanding the Hamas Massacre of October 7th, 2023

hear and speak the truth to those around them, who may be caught in a web of confusion and deceit.

Some believers wonder whether they should "stand by Israel" but are upset by the level of violence and the number of deaths in Gaza and are confused by reporting that has emphasized the suffering of the people of Gaza and has portrayed Israel as engaging in "genocide."

Background Perspective

First, perspective is necessary. There was peace in the region, and Israel allowed many inhabitants of Gaza to work in plentiful, well-paying jobs in Israel. Recently, they had greatly increased the number of guest workers allowed.[8]

There was a higher level of peace in the Middle East than at any earlier time, as Israel had signed peace treaties with several Arab states and was working towards a peace treaty with Saudi Arabia. Israel and the Saudis were talking of collaborating on a new trade route that would land goods on the Indian Ocean coast and then move them by train to Israel for trans-shipment around the world.

General peace and prosperity were on the rise in the region. Enemies of Israel and the West, including Iran and its proxies in Iraq, Syria, Lebanon, Gaza, the West Bank, and Yemen, were threatened by this peace.

---

[8] The role of the "guest workers" allowed into Israel is significant for two reasons: The first is that Israel was working toward allowing more of these workers in as a gesture of goodwill as well as the alleviation of the economic hardships on Gazan citizens because of the arms blockade imposed by Israel and Egypt on Gaza after the terrorist organization Hamas took over in 2007. The second reason why this is significant is that allegedly these guest workers were among those "civilians" who took part in the October 7th massacre. https://freebeacon.com/national-security/just-as-cruel-as-the-terrorists-many-ordinary-palestinians-joined-in-hamass-atrocities-against-israel/

October 7, 2023

Then, on October 7, 2023, a great evil was unleashed against Israel. Hamas launched a massive attack that overwhelmed border defenses and spread massive bloodshed and horrendous, unspeakable acts of violence in Israel. Hamas is a terrorist group that calls in its charter for the extermination of all Jews and the conquest of the entire land of Israel. They used information gleaned from guest workers and others to plan their assaults.

These attacks were designed to be as horrifying as possible – both to provoke an Israeli response and to unleash evil. Over 1,300 Israeli citizens and citizens of other countries were murdered. Many were tortured before being killed. Parents were forced to watch their infants being slaughtered before their eyes. Women were brutalized in unthinkable ways and then killed. More than 200 hostages were taken back into Gaza as trophies and to be used as human shields.

Responding to that pogrom-like attack – the most significant loss of Jewish life since the Holocaust – Israel determined to attack Hamas in Gaza with the twin goals of recovering the hostages and destroying Hamas' capability ever again to launch such an attack. The Israeli Defense Forces are still engaged in those actions, even as negotiations allowed the release of some hostages.

Five Principles

To truly grasp the significance of these horrific events, we need to understand five fundamental principles from God's word. We pray, "Thy Kingdom come, Thy will be done, on earth as it is in heaven." God has a plan for the earth and every life, but evil is real, and Satan is a real being who is opposed to God's work and wants to stop God's plans. We need to be aware of the supernatural battles happening all around us.

Chapter 2 Five Biblical Principles for Understanding the Hamas Massacre of October 7th, 2023

1. **God has a unique, irrevocable calling on the Jewish people, and He has stated that He will judge the nations and people according to how they treat Israel.**

God called Abram and covenanted with him to give him the land of Israel (Genesis 12-15). He further promised that all the nations of the earth would be blessed through the Jewish people and that whoever blessed Israel, God would bless, and whoever cursed Israel, God would curse. This promise is not just for the Jewish people, but according to God's own words, it will be through the Jewish people that "…and in you all the families of the earth will be blessed."

Jesus' word is true, "salvation is from the Jews." (John 4:22) This flies in the face of our humanism. It doesn't seem fair that God would favor one person or nation – but this is the truth God declared in his Word.

2. **History proves that Israel is not perfect and has fallen into sin, but that God's promises still apply to them. God judges Israel for her sins – but still judges those who curse her.**

We do not know why God allowed this attack to occur. But even so, there are things in Israel that displease God, and we do need to pray for repentance for Israel from those sins which beset her. Pray that they will turn and accept their Messiah, Yeshua (Jesus), and discover the new life and hope that He brings.

But Scripture is very clear that whenever nations are used to judge Israel, they themselves are also judged. (Joal 3:2) We need to pray for revival throughout the Middle East, and for reconciliation between the children of Isaac (Jews) and Ishmael (Arabs).

3. **The October 7 attack was Satanically inspired and directed. Satan desires to use it to provoke a genocide of the Jewish people, ignite a World War, and bring destruction and death to the whole earth.**

Satan has acted throughout history to oppose and try to kill the Jewish people. We see the supernatural plans of the devil in the centuries-long history of nation after nation trying to exterminate the Jewish people, though God has repeatedly brought them through.

These schemes are evident when we look at pogroms and blood libels throughout history. They can be seen in the book of Esther; in the events of the Spanish Inquisition (aimed mainly at the Jews); in the writings and actions of Hitler and the Holocaust; in Stalin's plans to eliminate the Jews in Russia; and in the wars that have beset Israel since their rebirth in 1948.

We see them today in the perverse accusations that Israel is committing genocide in Gaza, despite the fact that she is taking great care to warn civilians of danger, yet at the same time Hamas is not accused of genocide even though they openly call for it and were attempting to carry it out. Satan twists the truth and works to stop the plans of God.

He knows that when the Jewish people come to faith in Yeshua, as is foretold in the Bible, it will be "life from the dead" (Romans 11:15). Just as Satan inspired Herod to slaughter the children of Bethlehem in an attempt to kill Yeshua (Jesus) as an infant, so today he continues to stir up murderous hatred of the Jewish people.

4. Some human actions are both revelatory and catalytic. October 7 was such an event.

Some events are revelatory in that they reveal the deeper intentions of the people involved in them. Some events go beyond even the human actors to reveal either God's intentions behind human actions or the devil's presence at work. Such events will accelerate or spread those plans already set in motion by previous events.

These revelatory/catalytic events often mark the hinge points in human history. They lead to the fulfillment either of God's intentions, or of Satan's intentions. God's intentions result in

Chapter 2 Five Biblical Principles for Understanding the Hamas Massacre of October 7th, 2023

greater good for humanity, which includes life, justice, and prosperity. Satan's intentions result in greater evils, such as death, oppression, injustice, misery, and want.

When an idea or a vision (whether good or evil) is clothed in action it also has a catalytic effect, building the psychological and spiritual conditions within people that can draw them into taking part in fulfilling the vision that has been presented to them.

Actions that embody God's manifest presence and kingdom draw others into God's presence and plans and build faith. They also draw out from people what is good and noble, which is then energized by the presence of the Holy Spirit. We see this dynamic at work when good deeds and acts of kindness evoke similar sentiments in others and lead to more good deeds. We can see this in the outpouring of service and love that people worldwide have shown to support those displaced by the events of October 7 and to the soldiers of the Israeli military.

Similarly, evil actions have the catalytic potential to unleash greater evil. When a person or a group does something evil, their violent or dehumanizing acts, causing harm or death, can then spark further evil acts. We see this in the evil events of Kristallnacht in 1938, and in the October 7 Massacre. This vicious cycle of evil draws others into similar immoral and inhuman acts.

5. **Satan cloaks his actions so they are not easily understood or perceived.**

One other concept that we must recognize as we embark upon this task of discernment and prayer is that Satan will do everything possible to obscure and hide what he is up to in the world. We will refer to this as "demonic cloaking." This cloaking happens through all sorts of psychological and spiritual processes. Satan actively works to obscure and distort the truth and to hide his true intentions. This occurs through deliberate deception and through a highly effective process of warping what we perceive as real and genuine.

When we apply these biblical principles to the October 7 Massacre of Jews to discern what is actually taking place and what has been set in motion, we see we are contending with major demonic cloaking which is obscuring the true meaning of what took place. We see evidence of this cloaking for instance, in media reporting which focuses only on civilian casualties in Gaza, or in the UN's one-sided condemnations of Israel, without any reference to either the diabolical atrocities of the October 7 Massacre or to Hamas' proven practice of using captives and their own population as human shields.

We also see this cloaking at work in the removal of many of the appalling images that the Jihadists themselves posted on the internet boasting of their murder of Jews, thereby hiding the evidence. We see it in media reports that accept statistics and stories from Hamas uncritically while disputing or not presenting statements from the Israeli government. We also see this in operation across university campuses and major cities in the United States and Great Britain where massive outpourings of support for Hamas includes calling for Palestine to be established "From the River to the Sea," seemingly oblivious to the fact that this is a Hamas slogan which refers to the complete elimination of Israel.

We will be applying these five principles firstly in order to discern the significance of the October 7th Hamas Massacre of Jews, and secondly to receive guidance on how the Lord is calling us to cooperate with the Holy Spirit in advancing the Kingdom of God over the plans of Satan which have been unleashed in these events.

Summary: Pointers for Praying

As always, believers should allow their prayers to be directed by the Holy Spirit. Many of these points will be elaborated on the pages that follow, but these may serve as a "Heads Up." Therefore pray:

Chapter 2 Five Biblical Principles for Understanding the Hamas Massacre of October 7th, 2023

- That Satan's plans would be completely unmasked and become obvious to everyone.

- That people would speak up and come against the lies of the devil that are confronting them.

- That God, in His mercy, would stop the hands of evil men so that no further blood would be shed. That He would remove them from power and would remove the sources of funding that allow terrorist organizations such as Hamas, Hezbollah and the Houthis to operate, as that enables rogue nations like Iran to act against Israel and the nations that stand with her.

- That all people, but especially Christian believers, would understand God's plan and call for Israel and would pray for the Jewish people to come to faith in Christ.

- That Israel and the Jewish people would indeed come to faith in their Messiah, Yeshua.

- That God would bring reconciliation to the offspring of Isaac and Ishmael.

- That God would bring revival to the Arab world and to Iran.

- And most of all, that God's plan of worldwide revival would begin.

3

Exposing Two Expressions of the Antichrist Spirit: Islam and Marxism

The October 7th invasion of Israel (which was the anniversary of the 1973 Yom Kippur War) and the terrible acts of violence against innocent Jews were revelatory. They exposed for all with eyes to see that over the last fifty years there has been a relentless rise of powerful demonic strongholds. These strongholds are exposed first by the Islamic Jihadists who committed the atrocities. As they shouted "Allahu Akbar" (Allah is greater) they revealed that this stronghold was based on Islam and the example and words of their founder Mohammad. The shock troops were Hamas, but a hydra-headed monster stands behind them. Hamas is part of an axis of evil which includes Hezbollah, the Houthis, and others under the control and support of Iran. This is held together by the deception of Islamic ideology and is characterized by a hatred of Jews, Israel, and the West. It is primarily governed by the apocalyptic expectation that their Mahdi will bring the universal rule of Islam and calls Muslims to take part in making the way for his arrival by exterminating the Jews.

The other heads of this demonic stronghold are revealed by

Chapter 2 Five Biblical Principles for Understanding the Hamas Massacre of October 7th, 2023

those who celebrated the massacre of Jews and stood in solidarity with Hamas and Palestine. It was not only Muslims who marched on the streets of Western capitals, but also members of the radical left - various permutations of Marxist ideology. They expressed their support for the people of Palestine but in fact they were also supporting the Islamic fanatics who were embodying their goals of wiping Israel off the earth and exterminating Jews wherever they are.

These movements have divergent agendas and incompatible worldviews. But nevertheless, there is a convergence taking place around two core manifestations of hatred of Jews: the destruction of Israel, and the extermination of the Jewish people.

These diverse expressions supporting Hamas are united by a hatred of God as He has revealed Himself in the Bible, of the descendants of the seed of Abraham through Isaac and Jacob, and of those engrafted into the family of Abraham through faith in Yeshua/Jesus.

What I believe has been exposed is at least two, perhaps more, distinct manifestations of the antichrist spirit that is referred to in John 8:4. In the last days, which may very well be upon us, John describes the following vision:

> Then I saw a beast rising out of the sea, that had ten horns and seven heads. On his horns were ten royal crowns, and upon his heads were slanderous names. (Rev 13:1 TLV)

The seven heads indicate a multiplicity of Satan's manifestations on earth as the antichrist, and these are expressed as demonic strongholds. These have been embodied in the individuals around whom the stronghold has been formed. In the final days of the End Times, John observes that two of these heads will be manifested as two beasts which appear to be expressed through two demonically empowered people. I am not suggesting that the October 7th Massacre has revealed the literal two Beasts as foretold in

Revelation 13. However, we are certainly seeing what could be described as two distinct but interconnected heads of the antichrist spirit.

One head of the antichrist is embodied around Islamic jihadist ideologies. At this time in history this is rooted in the theocratic dictatorship of Iran which is expressed through its various proxies in the Jihadist movements of Hamas, Hezbollah, and the Houthis based in Yemen.

The second head of the antichrist is rooted in the various expressions of Marxism which are taking over many institutions in the West. They are embodied in globalism and have established their instrumentality in the World Economic Forum and the UN, as well as in many different movements such as Diversity, Equity and Inclusion (DEI) and intersectionality. All these have their roots in Marxist dialectic and the division of humanity into warring classes of the oppressed and oppressor.

The insane contradictions embedded in the cooperation between these two expressions of the antichrist (Radical Islam and Marxism) are noted by Alan Dershowitz:

> "Among the groups that have supported the rapes, beheadings mass murders and kidnapping of Jews by Hamas have been some that purport to speak for gays, Jews, feminists, and progressives. If any of these groups were actually to travel to Gaza, they would be murdered by Hamas, which has no tolerance for gays, Jews, feminists, or progressives. Indeed, among the people beheaded, raped, murdered, and kidnapped were gays, Jews who supported Palestinians, feminists, and progressives. None of that matters to Hamas. If you are a Jew or an Israeli, you are a target of their barbarity."[9]

These two expressions of the antichrist spirit have contradictory

---

[9] Dershowitz, Alan *War Against the Jews: How to End Hamas Barbarism*, Skyhorse Publishing, New York, pg. 60.

Chapter 2 Five Biblical Principles for Understanding the Hamas Massacre of October 7th, 2023

and, indeed, incompatible agendas. But they are united by a hatred of Jews and the common goal of destroying Israel. At their root, they are two expressions of the same Satan who hates the Sovereign God revealed in the Bible. These two strongholds, working in an evil alliance, have great power and reach, and are working globally to fulfill Satan's agenda of opposing the advancement of God's Kingdom.

The collusion between these demonic strongholds is contributing significantly towards obscuring the actual plans of Satan. The unholy alliance of these two strongholds is no doubt having a divisive effect on the leaders of Israel who have united to fight this war. It is also creating division and confusion among the leaders and political parties of its two most steadfast allies: The United Kingdom and the United States.

The revelatory events of October 7th are inflaming antisemitism and are bringing division and the unraveling of the Democratic Party in the United States. This is no longer the party of liberalism, but of radical leftism and wokeism, as well as an increasing hatred of Jews. This fracturing does not bode well for America's historical support of Israel and the Jewish people, or for liberal democratic values in America and worldwide.[10] So far, it is not clear how well the Republican party is doing in the face of this onslaught. There are tendencies toward what some have identified as Christian nationalism in the Republican party. There are tendencies toward isolationism, which would lead America to disengage from the world, especially when it comes to the complexity of the Middle East and threats against the Jewish people.

All this is to say that this two-headed expression of the antichrist was exposed by the October 7th Hamas Massacre of the Jews and by the repercussions it is having worldwide. It is also revealing that beyond the human realm there is an ominous stirring of the forces of darkness in the spiritual realm whose malevolent presence is

---

[10] Ibid. pg. 73-75 Dershowitz observes and documents this division within the Democratic Party.

being manifest through widespread expressions of hatred of the Jews and the calls for their extermination.

But is this analysis really the case? Is it true that the present-day Islamic and Marxist expressions of the antichrist are calling for genocide of an entire race? Do they genuinely mean to murder millions of human beings if they have the means to do so? We must address this subject head-on and not naively avoid it just because it is too horrible to contemplate. We address that question in the next chapter.

Summary: Pointers for Praying

A revelatory event reveals what is happening spiritually through unfolding physical events. Satan, in his empire of evil, is very skilled at hiding what he is doing so that the world remains unaware of his plans. We call this "demonic cloaking." But there are occasions when events unfold that reveal what is happening spiritually. This may happen through God's sovereign act, or as an answer to the prayers of intercessors praying for the piercing of demonic cloaking. These events can reveal elements of demonic strongholds that Satan is using to block and hinder God's Kingdom.

October 7 was a revelatory event in that it showed the demonic and barbaric heart at the center of Hamas. Evil was unleashed which seared the Israeli soul. Hatred and destruction of the Jews were revealed as part of a demonic stronghold, one which included Hamas, Hezbollah, the Houthis, and others under the support and control of Iran. It is a stronghold that had formed within the Shiite Islamic culture.

In the worldwide protests that followed, pro-Palestinian Muslim people came together with various radical leftist groups. Even

Chapter 2 Five Biblical Principles for Understanding the Hamas Massacre of October 7th, 2023

though these two groups have widely divergent worldviews and agendas, they coalesced around a common theme of hatred for the Jews and even justification for the assault on Israel on October 7th. These protests also revealed another stronghold of the Enemy that has established itself within Western culture and society. This stronghold, like the one based on Islam, has hidden behind many names such as "woke" and the "radical left," all of which are variations of the antichrist ideology of Marxism. These two strongholds, though very different in many respects, were overlapping and fusing together in their attitudes towards the Jews.

The problem is that many people are seemingly unable to notice what is taking place. They don't see the truth. As intercessors, our primary prayer strategy is to pray that any demonic cloaking is pierced. In praying this, we are asking that the truth be exposed. Therefore, pray that people would see clearly:

- The truth about the atrocities that occurred on October 7.

- The truth about the core hatred and agenda of Hamas.

- The truth about the support of the Iranian regime and the events that followed.

- The truth about the growing anti-Semitism worldwide.

- The truth that Satan, using fear and hatred, would also instigate incidents of Islamophobia.

- The truth that, because of October 7, there has been a stirring within the spiritual realm of evil, seeking to polarize, divide, spread hatred and fear, pushing the world towards a place of increased instability and chaos.

Intercessors need to continue to pray for the demonic cloaking to be pierced so that the motives and agendas of *everyone* involved are seen. This includes not only Hamas, Hezbollah and Iran, but also Israel, the United States, the United Nations, the United Kingdom, the European Union, as well as the other Middle Eastern Muslim states.

Pray that God's will would be done in these nations and that the Lord would constrain the forces of evil.

Chapter 2 Five Biblical Principles for Understanding the Hamas Massacre of October 7th, 2023

4

Extermination of the Jewish People—Really?

A deeply troubling revelation took place through the October 7th massacre and the response to it, namely the global rise and intensification of antisemitism, including calls for the destruction of Israel and the extermination of Jews. For clarity we are referring to this plainly as "Jew-hatred."

The extermination of an entire race of people is so utterly abominable, so horrible and abhorrent as to be unthinkable. This is especially so for any of us who have, seared into our hearts and minds, the images of what the extermination of entire peoples looks like from the Armenian Genocide or the Nazi Holocaust. Those historic events were like the actions seen in the images of the October 7th massacre, but multiplied in scale into unspeakable, unimaginable horror and unfathomable degrees of human suffering.

Those in power during past eras who failed to intervene to stop the Armenian Genocide or the Holocaust simply did not believe that such evil was possible. They could not accept that the Turks or the Nazis could implement such terrible evil, or that an entire society could become so deceived and be manipulated into taking part in such ghastly deeds. Part of the problem was that, although

Chapter 4 The Extermination of the Jewish People—Really?

those who perpetrated these monstrous crimes were saying that they would do them, very few people in that past era took them seriously. Like Hitler announcing his plans of a Europe *judenrein* (Jew free or cleansed of Jews) and advocating a "Final Solution of the Jewish Problem," Hamas, Hezbollah, and the Iranian Islamic dictators and a chorus of other Jew-haters, have consistently and repeatedly announced to the world their intentions to destroy Israel and exterminate the Jewish people. Such blindness was catastrophic in the 1930s and could be equally catastrophic today if we and the world are blind to the revelations and reverberations of October 7th.

To get past this blindness we must start by paying attention to what Hamas and their supporters are actually saying. Even before the IDF started its massive counterattack, protestors supporting Hamas against Israel were voicing calls for genocide of the Jews. As I looked closely at the protesters in many places around the world, they are chanting "gas the Jews," calling for a Holocaust 2.0 to complete the work of Hitler, and "from the river to the sea" calling for the eradication of Israel as a nation. It is incredible that these statements are being made. This was not just my reading into what I saw. Here are some following reports which back up this observation. These reports that there were those chanting "gas the Jews" were from the October 9th protest at the Sydney Opera House. I never saw that report until much later, what I saw were protests in other locations. Apparently, there is a dispute about whether this was what was actually chanted, which is not surprising. The Executive Council of Australian Jewry (ECAJ) co-CEO Alexander Ryvchin reaffirmed his belief in the witnesses who claimed to have heard the chants but stressed that the exact words "is not the core issue".

> "The core issue is that on October 9, before Israel had even commenced its military response, just two days after the greatest atrocity inflicted on the Jewish people since the Holocaust, a mob of thugs gathered at one of our nation's most cherished sites to celebrate the mass

slaughter and rape of Israelis, to burn Israeli flags and to chant threateningly towards fellow Australians..."

Further, that these protesters not just in Australia but other locations called for a repeat of the Nazi Holocaust is confirmed by other reports. One for instance is the fact that Jewish students sued NYU (New York University) claiming the university allows students to chant 'gas the Jews' - The Jewish Chronicle.[11] I seriously doubt that such a legal action would have been undertaken unless there really were these unambiguous calls for genocide of the Jews.

These calls for genocide confirm that demonically energized and politically manipulated Jew-hatred is taking place in many different locations and, ominously, on the elite college campuses of the United States, Canada and the United Kingdom. We have seen in the news reports the gatherings on many USA, Canadian and United Kingdom campuses in support of Hamas. Students of the most prestigious universities, who are supposed to be the beacons of Western civilization, are actually calling for, not just the destruction of Israel, but the extermination of the Jewish people.

These calls for the extermination of the Jews and the failure to condemn them was most graphically illustrated at a hearing in the United States House of Representatives on antisemitism in which the presidents of three prestigious American Universities – the University of Pennsylvania, Harvard, and MIT - were unable or unwilling to unequivocally repudiate calls for genocide of the Jews that occurred on their campuses. [12]

Here is a report from the BBC on the Congregational Hearing that was held on Tuesday, December 7th, 2023. University of

---

[11] *Jewish students sue NYU claiming university allows students to chant 'gas the Jews' Bella Ingber, Sabrina Maslavi and Saul Tawil accused the university of 'egregious civil rights violations' BY RICHARD PERCIVAL NOVEMBER 15, 2023* https://www.thejc.com/news/world/jewish-students-sue-nyu-claiming-university-allows-students-to-chant-gas-the-jews-omkrmkxw

[12] https://www.bbc.com/news/world-us-canada-67631228)

Chapter 4 The Extermination of the Jewish People—Really?

Pennsylvania President Elizabeth Magill and her MIT and Harvard counterparts were asked directly and repeatedly by Representative Elise Stefanik if calling for the genocide of Jews violated the code of conduct at their schools. All answered - in varying ways - that it depended on the "context".[13]

> "In an exchange that has now gone viral, Stefanik, a graduate of Harvard, pressed Elizabeth Magill, the president of UPenn, to say whether students calling for the genocide of Jews would be disciplined under the university's code of conduct."[14]

It was stunning to watch the weaseling way they dodged her direct questions about calls for genocide of the Jews. This congregational hearing reveals a great deal of the nature of the demonic strongholds of deception that have gained great power in many strategic locations including our prestigious universities.

When woke college students and college presidents like Dr. Gay of Harvard, who are promoting their agenda of diversity, equity, and inclusion (DEI), not only cannot reject calls for genocide of Jews but stand in solidarity with Hamas, then they are also culpable in the destruction of Israel and the genocide that is being called for. We shall show later that because they are cursing God's chosen people, that the Lord God has declared war against them as individuals, movements, and institutions.

---

[13] (https://www.bbc.com/news/world-us-canada-67631228)

[14] (https://www.theguardian.com/us-news/2023/dec/07/university-presidents-antisemitism-congress-testimony)

Does Islam really call for the extermination of Jews and Christians?

To grasp the deep origins of this call for genocide of the Jews, we must expose the demonic roots of both movements that are standing together in solidarity at this junction in history: the Islamic Jihadist and the Marxist radical left. However, it is beyond the narrow scope of this prayer guide to delve into the demonic roots of Marxism and the calls for the extermination of entire peoples in that antichrist ideology. I have written extensively in other publications on the evidence that Karl Marx was demonized. [15] Let us focus here on the bloody point of the spear—the Islamic jihadist terrorist movement named Hamas.

In order to understand the reality of intentions for genocide of Jews that was exposed in the October 7th Massacre, we must uncover the demonic roots of Islam. We must do this to avoid being deceived, as much of the world seems to be.

Social and political commentary interprets this war within the constraints of a merely worldly paradigm. It is perceived as a geopolitical conflict, a political struggle for a Jewish and a Palestinian state, a people's liberation movement against colonial oppression, or even as a defensive battle against the Jews who are alleged to be committing genocide against the innocent Palestinian people.

But if we listen to the Islamic Jihadists themselves, it is clear that they are deriving their mandate from Islam. This is plainly stated within their own charters. When they march on the streets in solidarity with members of the radical left, or argue their cause in America, Canada, or the UK, they couch their goals in terms that

---

[15] Rabbi Mark Rantz and I do that in our book on the *Exposing the Trojan Horse of the BLM Organization: Spiritual Warfare Strategies for Advancing the Kingdom of God*, there we demonstrate that not only did Karl Marx call for the extermination of entire peoples but that he was himself possessed by high level demons.

Chapter 4 The Extermination of the Jewish People—Really?

will be sympathetically understood by the extreme left and the Western worldview. But that is a smoke screen and a façade. As they mutilated, raped and murdered their victims their cry was not "Workers of the World Unite!" or "Liberate Palestine!" but was a relentless chant of "Allahu Akbar."

Therefore, the defining question we must ask is: does Muhammad the Prophet, and do the sacred texts of Islam, the Koran and Hadith, really advocate the murder of all unbelievers, and especially the Jewish people? I addressed this question exhaustively in my book, *Discerning the Times: Exposing Satan's Plans in Radical Islam.* Let me give you enough here to support my conclusion that there are indeed many words and actions of their prophet that support this conclusion.

Please note carefully that the issue is not whether this reflects true Islam or the beliefs and attitudes of all Muslims. The issue is that Satan has *used* these sacred texts and the actions of their prophet to create demonic strongholds to exterminate Jews and Christians. The same argument can also be made about how Satan used the words of the Holy Bible and those of the great reformer, Martin Luther, to create the demonic stronghold of Nazism in order to carry out his same plan of exterminating the Jews.

The quotes below are taken right out of the Koran. They are used to justify the atrocities of October 7th and provide the basis of the call for genocide for Jews and Christians. Furthermore, since these words are said to have "Allah's approval" when they are spoken or acted upon, they also function as curses against Jews and Christians. (Note that verses in the Koran are not in the form of narrative or letter, like most of the Bible, but are a list of statements, similar to the book of Proverbs.)

- "Kill the unbelievers wherever you find them." (Koran 2:191)
- "Make war on the infidels living in your neighborhood." (Koran 9:123)
- "When opportunity arises, kill the infidels wherever you catch them." (Koran 9:5)

- "Any religion other than Islam is not acceptable." (Koran 3:85)
- "The Jews and the Christians are perverts fight them..." (Koran 9:30)
- "Maim and crucify the infidels if they criticize Islam." (Koran 5:33)
- "Punish the unbelievers with garments of fire, hooked iron rods, boiling water melt their skin and bellies." (Koran 22:19)
- "The unbelievers are silly, urge the Muslims to fight them." (Koran 8:65)
- "Muslims must not take the infidels as friends." (Koran 3:28)
- "Terrorize and behead those who believe in scriptures other than the Qur'an." (Koran 8:12)
- "Muslims must muster all weapons to terrorize the infidels." (Koran 8:60)[16]

The final quote (below) is the hadith that has been often quoted and which is in the original Hamas charter:

- "Judgement Day will not come until the Muslims fight the Jews. The Jews will hide behind the stones and the trees, and the stones and the trees will say, oh Muslim, oh servant of Allah, there is a Jew hiding behind me — come and kill him."[17]

---

[16] I got this summary from the following site http://www.nairaland.com/1283381/these-verses-really-quran

[17] 'There is a Jew hiding behind me — come and kill him' "Judgement Day will not come until the Muslims fight the Jews." By Ben Cohen, September 24, 2021 https://jewishchronicle.timesofisrael.com/there-is-a-jew-hiding-behind-me-come-and-kill-him/ This hadith which is related by al-Bukhari and Moslem is given in Article Seven of the 1988 Hamas Charter. (pg. 152, Dershowitz, Alan, *War Against the Jews: How to End Hamas Barbarism*, Skyhorse Publishing. New York- 2023.)

Chapter 4 The Extermination of the Jewish People—Really?

The cumulative effect of these commands is a call to genocide first of Jews, then Christians, and all others deemed to be infidels. To liberal Western ears this seems bizarre, monstrous and unthinkable. Are there really leaders in the Islamic community who, on the basis of these texts, are genuinely advocating the extermination of whole races - the killing of all who do not convert to their creed or submit to being subjugated and humiliated? Can it really be that all this is taken seriously in the Muslim world and that there are those who are committed to carrying out this program? Do they really think that it comes from Allah, even though it breaks God's fundamental rule of "thou shall not murder" and bears all the marks of Satan?

The actions of Hamas Jihadists in the attacks of October 7th demonstrate that this call for genocide is taken seriously by some jihadist groups in Islam. The President of Egypt, Abdel Fattah el-Sisi, has acknowledged (and criticized the fact) that this is the understanding of jihadists.

In a remarkable speech given to Al-Azhar[18] and the Awqaf Ministry on New Year's Day, 2015, Sisi named and condemned these calls for genocide within Islam. At that time the specific concerns related to Islamic State, who have the same ideology and goals as Hamas. Here is the relevant excerpt from Sisi's speech (translation by Michele Antaki):

---

[18] Al-Azhar University (ahz-har; Arabic: جامعة الأزهر (الشريف) Jāmi'at al-Azhar (al-Sharīf), IPA: [ˈɡæmʕet elˈʔazhɑr eʃʃæˈriːf], "the (honorable) Azhar University") is a university in Cairo, Egypt. Founded in 970 or 972 by the Fatimids as a centre of Islamic learning, its students studied the Qur'an and Islamic law in detail, along with logic, grammar, rhetoric, and how to calculate the lunar phases of the moon. ...It is associated with Al-Azhar Mosque in Islamic Cairo. The university's mission includes the propagation of Islamic religion and culture. To this end, its Islamic scholars (ulamas) render edicts (fatwas) on disputes submitted to them from all over the Sunni Islamic world regarding proper conduct for Muslim individuals and societies. Al-Azhar also trains Egyptian government-appointed preachers in proselytization (da'wa). http://en.wikipedia.org/wiki/Al-Azhar_University

"I am referring here to the religious clerics. We have to think hard about what we are facing—and I have addressed this topic a couple of times before. *It's inconceivable that the thinking that we hold most sacred should cause the entire umma [Islamic world] to be a source of anxiety, danger, killing, and destruction for the rest of the world. Impossible!*

"That thinking—I am not saying "religion" but "thinking"—that corpus of texts and ideas that we have sacralized over the centuries, to the point that departing from them has become almost impossible, is antagonizing the entire world!

"Is it possible that 1.6 billion people [Muslims] should want to kill the rest of the world's inhabitants—that is, 7 billion—so that they themselves may live? Impossible!

I say and repeat again that we are in need of a religious revolution. You, imams, are responsible before Allah. The entire world, I say it again, the entire world is waiting for your next move... because this umma[19] is being torn, it is being destroyed, it is being lost—and it is being lost by our own hands.[20]"

I have included this in detail because it is so extraordinary! The President of Egypt is lecturing the preeminent Islamic University in

---

[19] Translators note: Note: It is unclear if in the last instance of umma Sisi is referring to Egypt ("the nation") or if he is using it in the pan-Islamic sense as he did initially to refer to the entire Islamic world.

[20] http://www.raymondibrahim.com/from-the-arab-world/egypts-sisi-islamic-thinking-is-antagonizing-the-entire-world

Chapter 4 The Extermination of the Jewish People—Really?

the world and those Islamic scholars[21] who are responsible for interpreting the Islamic texts and traditions. It is incredible that he would feel obliged to tell them such things! When President Sisi keeps saying that this is "Impossible," he is rejecting those calls for genocide that are evident in the texts of Islam and are upheld by these scholars.

Sisi draws attention, not to their religion but to their "thinking," i.e. the body of texts and ideas that, over time, have come to be regarded as sacred. This thinking includes the genocide of Jews, Christians, and everyone else who is not Muslim. This, he says, is antagonizing the entire world.

President Sisi himself does not attribute this "thinking" or system of thought to demonic origins. However, Satan, the Father of Lies, has indeed built a stronghold of lies in the minds and hearts of human beings. These are systems of thought (Paul calls them "arguments") that are false and are opposed to the Truth of God that is made known through general revelation through nature and reason, and special revelation in the Holy Bible especially in Jesus Christ. (2 Cor 10:3-5).

President Sisi sees that embedded within this thinking, based on the sacred text of Islam, is the intention to kill the rest of the world's inhabitants. This is the basis of the demonic stronghold that Satan has built to exterminate the Jewish people.

These plans for genocide were vividly exposed in the October 7th Hamas Massacre of Jews. Satan is using specific sacred Islamic texts and certain groups within the Muslim world to accomplish the plans for genocide, starting with Jews and then Christians and everyone else. If this really is true, and I hope that all those who read this are now persuaded that it is, then we must take the calls

---

[21] Ulama (Arabic: علماء 'Ulamā', singular عالِم 'Ālim, "scholar"), also spelled ulema, alimah (female) and "uluma", in contemporary usage by Muslims refers to the religious elite of scholars at the top of the sectarian hierarchy. They mainly specialize in fiqh (Islamic jurisprudence) and are considered the arbiters of sharia law by mainstream sects; however, their authority is not universally accepted (See Controversial Aspects). http://en.wikipedia.org/wiki/Ulama

for genocide with the utmost seriousness and do everything possible to prevent it from taking place.

Later in this book we shall consider how the Lord God is calling us to take part in stopping Satan's plans. But before we can get there, we must go deeper still and ask the question of "Why?" Why is there this unified call for the destruction of Israel and the genocide of Jews by groups with extremely different ideological and spiritual roots? To answer to this urgent question of "why," we must step back from the fog of war and clashing opinions and seek clarity by understanding Satan's grand schemes and ultimate objectives. However, we cannot comprehend the rationale for Satan's strategies until we understand God's masterplans for His Kingdom. The next chapter provides an overview of God's salvation plans which, fundamentally, started with and continue to include the Jews, the Land of Israel, and Jerusalem.

Summary: Pointers for Praying

The battle that we are fighting is primarily a spiritual one. While we see the reality and physical expressions, the principal battlefront is spiritual. Satan is using Islamic texts to promote the destruction of Israel and the Jewish people. The rapid expansion in antisemitic expression suggests that this antisemitic mindset is being demonically energized. How can we pray?

- Pray for a revelation of the truth that the goal of Hamas is genocide. While this truth is being spoken, the enemy clouds people's eyes so they cannot see (2 Corinthians 4:4), so pray that the Light of the truth would shine brightly and dispel the darkness and lies of the enemy.

A common enemy tactic is to project what he is doing onto other

Chapter 4 The Extermination of the Jewish People—Really?

people so that they appear to be doing evil. We see this with the accusations of genocide that are continually addressed towards Israel. There has been a significant loss of Palestinians' lives in this current conflict, but the stated goals of Israel are not genocide whereas those are the explicit goals of Hamas.

- Pray for an end to the projection of genocide intent onto Israel, and for the deep roots and goals of Hamas to be recognized.

A vital aspect of this battle is propaganda, primarily done through social media. Social media is not always factual.

- Pray that people would see through the deceptive narratives on social media and seek the truth.

- Pray for the clear presentation of truth by news media and government spokespeople.

- Pray for the victims of these lies, for both the Palestinian and Israeli peoples who are in distress, as they experience a variety of different emotional, mental, and physical stresses as well as spiritual trauma and pain.

- Pray for God's presence and grace, and that through all that is happening, hearts will turn to the Lord.

5

God's Master Plans for His Kingdom to Come

We must, for a moment, step out of this process of pondering what Satan is doing, which is all awful and unthinkable, and fix our eyes firmly on God the Father and His master plans. We must do this to ensure that we do not lose sight of our overall task, which is to pray and work for the Gospel of Jesus Christ to go to all nations. It is dangerously easy to get so distracted in fighting the devil and defeating these plans for genocide that we lose our focus on God and His Kingdom. In facing down genuine Goliaths, we must never forget that the battle belongs to the Lord!

If we are to understand the deep rationale behind Satan's recurring strategy of exterminating the Jews, then we must gain the big picture of God's master redemptive plans. And if we are to understand Satan's timing for his attacks then we must grasp the big picture of how, in our epoch, God's salvation plans are reaching fulfillment in historically unprecedented ways.

A comprehensive description of God's plans for the salvation of fallen humanity is way beyond the scope of this present book. But some key elements are essential for understanding why this curse of genocide of the Jews has been launched and is spreading worldwide through the contagion of Jew-hatred.

Acts 1:4-8 Launching the Two Streams of the Holy Spirit Advancing God's Kingdom Vision

Let us affirm as a foundation the fact that God chose the Jewish people as the means for bringing salvation to fallen humanity. This is firmly established in the calling of Abraham and his response of faith and obedience. God determined that all the families of earth will be blessed through his descendants. This stream has been fulfilled in the coming of Jesus Christ, and it is through Jesus and faith in Him that both individuals and the nations receive the blessing of life entry into God's Kingdom and eternal life.

> Just as Moses lifted up the serpent in the desert, so the Son of Man must be lifted up, so that whoever believes in Him may have eternal life! "For God so loved the world that He gave His one and only Son, that whoever believes in Him shall not perish but have eternal life." (John 3:14-16 TLV)

The converse is also true; those who do not believe in Jesus the Messiah do not have eternal life but perish and fall under God's judgment.

> "Now this is the judgment, that the light has come into the world and men loved the darkness instead of the light, because their deeds were evil. For everyone who does evil hates the light and does not come to the light, so that their deeds will not be exposed. But whoever practices the truth comes to the light, so that it may be made known that his deeds have been accomplished in

God." (John 3:19-21 TLV)

The book of Acts reveals that God the Father has chosen to spread this Gospel of Salvation through the outpouring of His Holy Spirit. The first outpouring took place in Jerusalem among Jesus' first believers, who were all Jewish, and then later spread in successive outpourings of the Holy Spirit, moving beyond the geographic limits of Jerusalem to other regions and to the nations. This spread included first the Samaritans, and then those who were non-Jews but were engrafted through faith in Jesus the Messiah into God's kingdom family.

God's grand plan of salvation for fallen humanity is encapsulated by Jesus' command given to his first disciples after his resurrection from the dead and before He ascended into heaven where, in his coronation as King of Kings, He received all authority in heaven and on earth. The command is this:

> Now while staying with them, He commanded them not to leave Jerusalem, but to wait for what the Father promised—which, He said, "you heard from Me. For John immersed [baptized] with water, but you will be immersed [baptized] in the Ruach ha-Kodesh [Holy Spirit] not many days from now." So when they gathered together, they asked Him, "Lord, are You restoring the kingdom to Israel at this time?" He said to them, "It is not your place to know the times or seasons which the Father has placed under His own control. But you will receive power when the Ruach ha-Kodesh [Holy Spirit] has come upon you; and you will be My witnesses in Jerusalem, and through all Judah, and Samaria, and to the end of the earth." Acts 1:4-8 TLV

Embedded in Acts 1:4-8 is a profound revelation of God the Father's means and strategic plans for our redemption. The first part concerns God's chosen people, the Jews, symbolized by two olive trees in Zechariah's vision (Zechariah 4:11). The second part

Chapter 5 God's Master Plans for His Kingdom to Come

of God's redemptive plan includes the non-Jewish peoples, the Gentiles or "wild olive tree" whom God the Father is engrafting into His original covenant people, the Jews (Rom 11:17) through Jesus Christ. Both great streams are launched by the power of the Holy Spirit poured out at Pentecost in Jerusalem. [22]

The Jewish stream is embodied in the expectation that the Kingdom will be restored to Israel and in their being empowered to witness to Yeshua "in Jerusalem, and through all Judah, and Samaria." This move God is expanded to include the non-Jewish Gentile stream, included in the disciples also being empowered to witness to Jesus Christ "to the ends of the earth."

In Acts 15, we find that it is God's plans and intention that these two streams are to be independent but nevertheless intermingled and mutually supported. This meant that the only way into the Kingdom of God was through faith in Jesus Christ. However, those who are part of the Jewish stream retain their Jewish roots and identity, while the non-Jews did not need to become Jews. The Jewish stream, together with the non-Jewish stream, become the "One New Man" in Christ as described in Ephesians 2:13-22.

In God's vision, both Jew and Gentile, as distinct but mutually supportive intermingled streams, will be working together as the "One New Man." This started in Jerusalem during the first Pentecost among the Jewish believers (Acts 2), and then continued in Caesarea, among the Gentile believers (Acts 10). Both outpourings launched great waves of the Holy Spirit, which were God the Father's means of fulfilling His redemptive plans for all humanity. These waves of the Holy Spirit have been sweeping around the world and, as they return to Jerusalem where they began, they will result in the "restoration of all things" promised in Acts 3:21: "This one [i.e. Jesus] heaven must receive until the time all things are restored, which God declared from times long ago

---

[22] To learn more about the reconnection between Jew and Gentile, check out Reconnecting Ministries and the Romans 911 Project at
https://reconnectingministries.org/romans-911/

through his holy prophets." This restoration of all things takes place through three strands: the Jews coming to faith in Jesus the Messiah; the kingdom being restored to Israel; and the gospel being preached to all the Gentile nations.

> Therefore, repent and turn back so that your sins may be wiped out, so that **times of refreshing** may come from the presence of the Lord, and so that he may send the Messiah appointed for you—that is, Jesus. This one heaven must receive until the time **all things are restored**, which God declared from times long ago through his holy prophets. (Acts 3:18-21)

The second great stream of the Holy Spirit launched with the fulfillment of Acts 1:4-8 is the Gentiles, which includes all the nations of the world who are the "wild olive branch," grafted into the Jewish trunk through Jesus Christ/Yeshua Ha Mashiach. This great move of God, which started in Jerusalem with the Jewish people, moved first within the Jewish world into Judea and Samaria and then, starting with the Holy Spirit falling upon the Roman Centurion Cornelius in Acts 10-11, moved to the rest of non-Jewish humanity (Romans 11:17).

Through faith in Jesus Christ the non-Jewish believers, the Gentiles, were grafted into God's covenants made with the Jewish people. This is the same basis upon which the Jews were joined into the New Covenant—faith in Jesus, who provided the way of salvation through His crucifixion, resurrection, ascension, and coronation as King.

Chapter 5 God's Master Plans for His Kingdom to Come

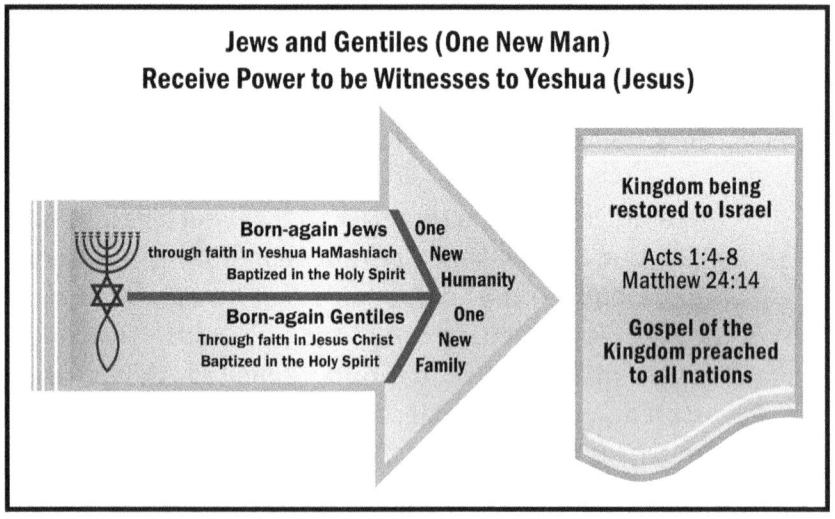

The diagram above represents the vision of how all this was to take place. However, the history is very different. First, there were Jews who did not receive Yeshua as the Messiah. Second, there was a major breach between the born again Jewish and Gentile believers in Jesus Christ. This took place through a long and terrible history which consisted of the Gentile stream essentially rejecting the Jewish side of the family and regarding themselves as the replacement for it. Throughout history there were many Jews who did accept Jesus Christ as Lord and Savior and were born again into the Kingdom of God. But they were repeatedly required to reject and give up their Jewishness. Worse still, there was the sowing of seeds of deep hatred and persecution of the Jewish people by the church of Jesus Christ. This fueled this division and made mutual appreciation and cooperation nearly impossible. This tragic antagonism has been used by Satan to cripple the advancement of the Gospel.

Over the last three hundred years the healing and restoration of these two branches of God's family has begun, starting with the outpourings of the Holy Spirit in the Moravian revival in 1727. Nicolaus Ludwig, Count Zinzendorf, welcomed Jewish believers who were born again through faith in Jesus Christ and were baptized with the Holy Spirit, but he did not require them to give up their Jewishness. In fact, Zinzendorf went the other extreme for a short season, requiring Moravian communities to eat kosher![23]

Now in this second decade of the 21st century, we are witnessing the fulfillment of Biblical prophecies that are markers of the End Times restoration of all things through Jesus the Messiah. The Jews are now returning to the Land of Israel and are returning to faith in Yeshua the Messiah. Born again Jews and Gentiles are now cooperating in empowered ministry to advance the Kingdom of God. This remarkable restoration of the family of God is depicted in the following chart prepared by Grant Berry of Reconnecting Ministries and the Romans 911 Project.[24]

---

[23] ZINZENDORF AND THE MORAVIANS: MESSIANIC TRAILBLAZERS - ONE FOR ISRAEL https://www.oneforisrael.org/bible-based-teaching-from-israel/zinzendorf-the-messianic-trailblazer/

[24] https://reconnectingministries.org/

Chapter 5 God's Master Plans for His Kingdom to Come

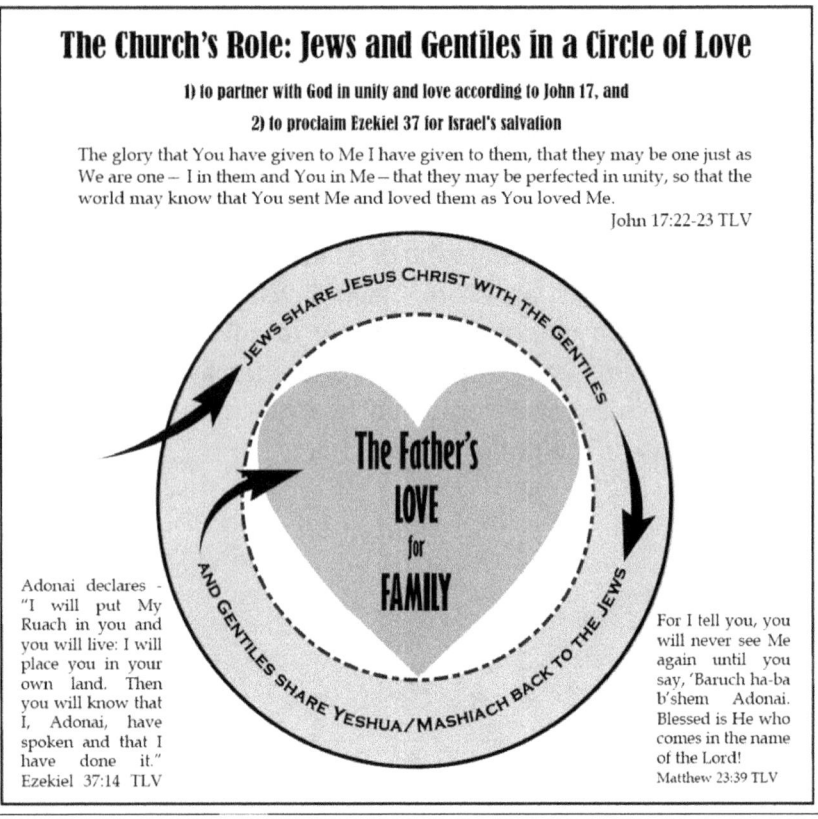

In this vast plan of God, when the nations are reached with the gospel of Yeshua Ha Mashiach/Jesus Christ and the Jewish people come to salvation through Yeshua Ha Mashiach/Jesus Christ, we shall see the "restoration of all things" in the return of Jesus Christ! This is affirmed by Yeshua/Jesus himself when he provides the final condition for His return: "This Good News of the kingdom shall be proclaimed in the whole world as a testimony to all the nations, and then the end will come" (Matt. 24:14 TLV). Paul confirms the role of the Jewish people coming to faith in Yeshua the Messiah as a decisive sign of the End Times.

> "For if their rejection leads to the reconciliation of the world, what will their acceptance be but life from the dead?" (Romans 11:15 TLV)

Now, when we consider that all these things are taking place right now, and that we are experiencing outpourings of the Holy Spirit in many locations worldwide, is it any wonder that Satan is especially active? He is creating the conditions to block this great move of God that is leading to the return to Jesus Christ, which marks Satan's downfall. This now makes sense of why, at this time, we are facing massive satanic counter attacks, starting with the threats of the destruction of Israel and the genocide of the Jewish people.

The fact that God's salvation plans are approaching the point of fulfillment is what provides the rationale for Satan's strategies and their timing. Having established this foundational understanding, let us now look at the question of timing, "why now?" Why did the October 7th Hamas Massacre of Jews take place at this moment in history, propagating worldwide this plague of Jew-hatred and curses of genocide, starting with the Jews but also including a large portion of the human family?

Chapter 5 God's Master Plans for His Kingdom to Come

6

Why Now, in the 2020s, Is Jew-hatred on the Rise?

Having provided this brief summary of God's master plans for redemption, and how they are taking place right now, we are ready to consider answers to some urgent questions. First now? Why did the October 7th Hamas Massacre of Jews take place when it did? Why has this event catalyzed Jew-hatred and calls for the extermination of the Jews worldwide now in 2024? Why are a number of hotspots around the world reaching boiling point, which, under the right conditions, could ignite a global war? Why is all this happening now in 2024? And second, what is Satan's true master strategy.

Why Now?

There have been many responses to this question "Why now?", which I will not elaborate on here.[25] Some have merit, others do

---

[25] There are many factors that do provide us with answers to this question of why now - some political and geopolitical. For instance, Caroline Glick, who is a

Chapter 6 Why Now, in the 2020s, Is Jew Hatred on the Rise?

not. I encourage you to review these different perspectives, as there are multiple layers. Here I am presenting my own interpretation, which draws on these others, but which is based also on the history of revivals and the expectation that we are in a time of impending great awakening.

> "Satan's actions may be understood as counteractions to the actions of God."

Jewish commentator, always gives deep insights into the politics of Israel and the USA. Her recent interview on her show with Victor Davis Hanson is profound and points out the role of the Radical Left as well as geopolitics: *Victor Davis Hanson: Hamas & Hezbollah believe US will not help Israel | The Caroline Glick Show* https://www.youtube.com/watch?v=I56vB3fn3ck
From the spiritual perspective I believe that these events are working out the consequences of the demonic invasion of the United States, that took place from 2020-2021. See my book *Days of Infamy* which can be obtained from the PRMI USA office prmi@prmi.org and our commentary from our prayer engagements - https://discernwith.us/prayer-communique
 In addition to the geopolitical explanations there has been much speculation of the spiritual causes of the Massacre. For instance, Rabbi Jonathan Cahn notes that it is 50 years after the Yom Kipper War and is all foretold in Biblical prophecy. https://www2.cbn.com/news/israel/jonathan-cahn-says-ancient-biblical-mystery-foretold-hamas-invasion-what-bible-says . A Hamas spokesman justified the attack by noting Israel had found the Red Heifers without blemish, which was a sign the Jews were about to offer sacrifices on the Temple Mount. https://www.jewishpress.com/news/israel/temple-mount-har-habayit/hamas-spokesman-abu-ubaydah-reveals-we-attacked-after-the-jews-imported-red-heifers/2024/01/26/ Others see this as the beginning of the fulfillment of End Times prophecy: American evangelicals interpret Israel-Hamas War as a prelude to End Times—Armed conflicts involving Israel are often associated with End Times' battles by American evangelicals, as many believe the Jewish state will play a role in fulfilling the biblical prophecy. November 17, 2023
By Fiona André https://religionnews.com/2023/11/17/american-evangelicals-are-interpreting-the-israel-hamas-war-as-a-prelude-to-end-times/

For an answer to this question, we need another discernment principle, which is summed up as follows: "Satan's actions may be understood as counteractions to the actions of God." Another way to put this is often phrased by my friend Steve Aceto, "When Jesus comes to town, the religious leaders get jealous, and the demons manifest."

All through the Bible, we find that the sovereign Lord God takes the initiative to advance His Kingdom on earth and that Satan, in response to God's redemptive plans, reacts against God's actions in order to oppose, subvert, and divert His plans for evil purposes. The religious leaders do indeed get jealous, trying to oppose God's work, and the demons certainly do manifest their presence.

An Old Testament example of Satan's counterattack to God's actions is the account in Exodus 17 of how the Amalekites attacked the Hebrews. The Hebrews were exhausted and vulnerable after the great miracles of the Exodus from bondage in Egypt and the miraculous provision in the wilderness. Seeking to take advantage of this vulnerable state, the Amalekites attacked. However, this counteraction by Amalek was followed by the battle in which Joshua prevailed over them on the battlefield as Moses, Aaron, and Hur were on the mountain engaged in intercessory prayer.

We see Satan's counterattack again clearly when Jesus, the anointed Messiah, came to Jerusalem for the Passover celebrations. Satan's counterattack was mediated through the Jewish religious leaders and Roman authority and resulted in his crucifixion.

Another example comes after the outpouring of the Holy Spirit at Pentecost that resulted in signs and wonders and the miracle of God adding to the number of believers, as recorded in Acts 2 and 3. Satan's counterattacks follow this in the form of threats that are described in Acts 4:3,18 and 21: "they grabbed them and put them in jail until the next day... they called them in and ordered them not to speak or teach at all in the name of Yeshua/Jesus. After threatening them again, they let them go."

The first disciples responded by crying out to God, praying for boldness and for the Lord to move in signs and wonders. The Lord

Chapter 6 Why Now, in the 2020s, Is Jew Hatred on the Rise?

responded by sending another outpouring of the Holy Spirit, pushing back their enemies, and empowering them for witness.

There are many historical examples of this principle. To name just one: The decade of 1900 to 1910 saw great global revivals ignited through R.A. Torrey, which were countered by Satan with the occult revival in Germany. This contributed towards igniting the First World War, with immense and insane slaughter on the battlefields of Europe, the Armenian genocide by Germany's allies, and the Islamic jihad by Ottoman Turks, as well as the Spanish flu pandemic. Satan's countermoves to God's revival left millions dead, wrecked nations, and spawned the antichrist ideologies of radical Islam, Bolshevism, and Nazism.

To see this dynamic at work, one does not have to look only to history and global events. It is our repeated experience in PRMI that, whenever there has been a manifestation of God's presence advancing His Kingdom, there is always a countermovement by Satan. For instance, in January of 2024 we had our PRMI Board Meeting and the annual gathering of the Dunamis Fellowship International. These were amazing events in which we celebrated the outpouring of the Holy Spirit that had taken place in multiple parts of the world. We also experienced the presence of the Holy Spirit as we looked to the future. We had a large delegation from Korea, representatives from the Chinese stream of PRMI, and representatives from our different branches in the USA, Canada, United Kingdom. We welcomed Messianic Jews, Roman Catholics, Reformed Presbyterians, and others! This was indeed a multinational gathering. Our theme was Unity in the Spirit, and we truly experienced this unity in Jesus!

But no sooner was the event over when members, the team and guests remaining onsite at the Community of the Cross came under major demonic attack. This unity that we had experienced so wonderfully during the Dunamis Fellowship International gathering was shattered. There was a major breakdown in our communication and relationships. It was a big mess that we had to work and pray our way out of. Counter moves of Satan against the great moves of God take place on deep personal levels as well as on the national and global levels.

Satan is Responding to the Fulfillment of God's Salvation Plans

Applying this discernment rule to the October 7th massacre places this terrible event within the larger context of God's redemptive plans and Satan's opposing countermoves. This biblical perspective helps us see that, over this last decade, there have been great outpourings of the Holy Spirit worldwide and Jews have been coming to faith in Yeshua, and there have also been radical actions in the geopolitical realm. For instance, President Trump moving the American Embassy from Tel Aviv to Jerusalem was an action that acknowledged what had been established by God's eternal decrees in the Bible – that Jerusalem is the true center of the Jewish people and the spiritual center of Israel.

A further positive indicator –as the signing of the Abraham Accords, in which Sunni Muslim states were moving from their traditional role of cursing Israel and the Jewish people and starting to take part in actually blessing them. This move from cursing to blessing was beginning to include even Saudi Arabia. This was a start that would bring God's blessing for these states and for Israel, especially in the human and material realms.

Above all, there has been genuine progress in fulfilling God's promises of Jeremiah 3. The Jews are returning to the Land and the Messianic movement is growing worldwide and in Israel with Jews accepting Yeshua as Lord and Savior. Through ministries such as Tikkun, these Messianic Jews are being brought into the Baptism with the Holy Spirit and becoming empowered witnesses to Yeshua.

Further, within the international church there is movement toward overcoming "replacement theology" and fulfilling the vision of the One New Man working together. God is in the process of restoring the Kingdom to Israel and is advancing the Gospel of the Kingdom to all nations.

Already, there is clear evidence of Jerusalem becoming the "throne of Adonai and that all nations will enter into it."

Chapter 6 Why Now, in the 2020s, Is Jew Hatred on the Rise?

Just look back at these last ten years leading up to the 2020s. We are in a time in which there is major advancement of the Gospel of Jesus Christ. We are at the beginning of what many are convinced is a global revival, one that could lead to the next Great Awakening which completes the Great Commission.

A unique and unprecedented aspect of this present great move of the Holy Spirit which is in continuity with the Great Moravian revival, is the present day fulfillment of the prophetic hope of born-again Jews and born-again Gentiles working together as the One New Man to advance the Kingdom. Resulting in what has always been the lofty ideal of the church embodied in Paul's vison, becoming a lived reality.

> There is neither Jew nor Greek, there is neither slave nor free, there is neither male nor female—for you are all one in Messiah Yeshua. And if you belong to Messiah, then you are Abraham's seed—heirs according to the promise. (Gal 3:28-29 TLV)

There is no room to go into all this positive good news of the great moves of the Holy Spirit that are presently taking place. I am convinced that, in our epoch, we are standing on the verge of the greatest revival of all time, one which could be the end times revival which completes the Great Commission and prepares for the return of Jesus Christ in glory.[26]

My conclusion is that the events of October 7th, 2023, were both revelatory and catalytic. They revealed Satan's plans for genocide of the Jewish people, and they also set them in motion. It was an attempt to stop this great move of God that is taking place. For only the second time in history, born-again Jews and born-again non-Jews are working together in the power of the Holy Spirit as the

---

[26] I document this great move of God that is taking place in my recent book entitled *Igniting Revivals in the Power of the Holy Spirit: The Bible Keys to Great Moves of God*.

One New Man, praying-in the Kingdom of God.

The first-time born-again Jews and Gentiles were together was soon after Pentecost, as recorded in Acts 15, which launched the global advancement of the Kingdom of God. This happened again in the Moravian revival that began in the 1720s. And it is happening once more in this epoch as a result of the decades of revivals starting around 1900. Today there are countless tributaries of revival in multiple nations and people groups, all merging together as a great river of God and reaching the tipping point of the Jews returning to faith in Yeshua and the Gospel of the Kingdom being preached to all nations.

Satan's Plans are to Stop This Great Outpouring of the Holy Spirit.

Satan's plan is to stop this remarkable outpouring of the Holy Spirit from spreading and igniting the exponential growth of the Kingdom of God that will occur as more and more people are born again through faith in Jesus and receive the baptism of the Holy Spirit. This move of the Holy Spirit is creating a tsunami of the love and presence of God to bring healing to the nations and to bring millions into God's eternal kingdom through faith in Jesus.

It is therefore no surprise that Satan is once again sending waves of hatred from the depths of hell, starting first with the Jews but then sowing discord and division throughout the entire human family. It is no surprise that Satan plans to destroy Israel and exterminate the Jewish people as well as all those who are gathering in Jerusalem in the name of Jesus Christ.

To achieve his terrible goals Satan is willing to murder millions of Jews and fling the entire world into a catastrophic war. He attempted this before in the 1930s and is trying it again in this present decade of the 2020s.

This is the reality that we face, and I believe that Jesus Christ is calling His church to arise. He is calling His Holy Spirit-empowered intercessors, as the vanguard, into the work of cooperation with God the Father, Son, and Holy Spirit to stop Satan's plans that have been exposed and set in motion through the October 7th Hamas Massacre of Jews.

This has been a lengthy, but necessary, introduction. The rest of this book will focus on the specific strategies and tactics of intercession and spiritual warfare that the Lord God is urgently calling His Church to deploy. Working through our faithful and Holy Spirit led actions, the Lord may not only hinder Satan's genocidal plans, but also continue to make way for the most significant revival of all times, leading to the restoration of all things through Jesus Christ.

Summary: Pointers for Praying

It is easy to become anxious and demoralized by the state of our world. The number of conflicts that are happening, the rise of anti-Semitism, and polarization in our society are all troubling. We can see the enemy's work and agenda and become overwhelmed. But when we remember all this is a reaction to what the Lord is doing, it helps us to gain perspective and gives us hope.

The task of intercession involves praying *for* the work that the Lord is doing and praying *against* the work the enemy is doing. As we continue in this book, we will increasingly focus on praying against the enemy's work. But before we do that, let us pray for the work that God is doing.

- Lord, thank you for the outpourings of the Holy Spirit that equip people to be witnesses for Jesus and ignite churches in their mission to fulfill the Great Commission

- Lord, we pray for more outpourings of your Holy Spirit that may lead to waves of revival.

- We praise you for moving in the hearts and lives of many Muslims. Thank you for the growing number of believers in Iran, Afghanistan, and other Muslim nations. Continue to draw people to the light of your truth.

- Thank you for drawing Jews to faith in your Son as their Messiah. Bless the growing Messianic Jewish communities in Israel and worldwide.

- We praise You for acting upon Your word and faithfully answering Your people's prayers. We pray that you will continue to give people a heart for intercession and that your Holy Spirit will guide and empower the work of prayer.

- Lord, we pray that you will continue to bless us with ever-increasing faith, hope, and love as we fix our eyes upon Jesus and follow Him.

7

Exposing Satan's Use of Curses to Dethrone God

Satan is seeking to block this great move of the Holy Spirit and to destroy the root of this cooperation between Jew and Gentile. He is seeking to block the fulfillment of God's plans, the restoration of all things in Jesus Christ. We see this taking place. The question which we must go deeper into now is: how does Satan intend to accomplish his abominable plans? This inquiry is not to satisfy our curiosity, but to prepare us to cooperate with the Holy Spirit in defeating these tactics.

How Satan Uses Curses to Accomplish His Purposes

In the spiritual realm these calls for the genocide of the Jews, either by protesters or prestigious university presidents who were unwilling to unconditionally condemn these calls, have become curses in Satan's hands which are used to accomplish his evil

Chapter 7 Exposing Satan's Use of Curses to Dethrone God

schemes.

To understand how Satan works, we must first understand how God works. God works on earth through His Word, written or spoken, and when received in faith, is embodied in actions and empowered by the Holy Spirit to accomplish the intent of His words. There are many examples of how this dynamic worked in the Bible. One example is when Mary received the word of an angel that she would conceive Jesus by the Holy Spirit. She received this in faith, and it took place.

A similar spiritual dynamic is at work with Satan, who is a spirit and, like God, must also work within the human sphere. Satan's words, which transmit his intentions, are spoken or written through his agents who receive them in faith and embody them in actions; they thus become the means by which those plans are implemented.

We see this satanic dynamic at work on October 7th when the Islamic Jihadists embodied the word of Satan. These evil words are actually written in the original charter of Hamas, which is faithful to the Koran and to the Hadith, calling for Muslims to murder Jews. They slaughtered Jews and were proud of it, and then sent their terrible images of their beheaded, tortured, and raped victims throughout the world. These images, and the calls to kill more Jews, functioned as curses that were demonically energized to advance Satan's plans.

What these Jihadists are enacting and celebrating is also the fulfillment of the curses already spoken by their prophet, Mohammad, such as, "Terrorize and behead those who believe in scriptures other than the Qur'an." (Koran 8:12)

By their acts of violence and hatred, they prove they are following the example of Mohammed in obedience to the Koran. Satan is now using the combination of the words of the Koran, together with images and videos of the "true Muslim" carrying out those words, as a curse to build faith in Islam and release even more evil. Satan then uses these curses and the faith they generate to deceive other Muslims into his demonic strongholds. The result is that both the individuals and the organizations are given demonic and earthly power to carry out Satan's purposes. Like a raging forest fire, it forms a vortex of evil which grows larger and larger by sucking more and more fuel into itself.

Today, as these curses are communicated through the internet and also through the network of demons within the spiritual realm, they begin to shape not only individual human hearts but the ethos or zeitgeist. This, in turn, results in putting in place the human power structures needed to carry out Satan's plans.

These dynamics are illustrated in the case of Hamas today and of Nazi Germany yesteryear. Genocide does not start in the actions of beheading Jewish children and raping women as on October 7th, or herding trainloads of Jews into gas chambers during the Holocaust. Genocide starts in the hearts of people who have given themselves over to hatred which is based on Satan's lies. Hatred always opens the door to the devil. When Gazan citizens cheer for the Jihadists and celebrate the murder of Jews, they open themselves to the demonic powers of death. When protesters join in the slogans calling for genocide or stand in solidarity with those whose purpose is mass murder, they also open themselves to the demonic powers of death.

These people are then led into incremental actions that collectively result in horrific crimes such as the Armenian Genocide, the Holocaust, or the October 7th massacre of innocent people.

Curses Removing the Land that God Promised to the Jews

Curses spoken by Jew-haters around the world are used by Satan in an effort to counter and destroy the covenant basis of bringing salvation to humanity. This system of Covenants revealed in the Holy Bible begins with the Noahic Covenant which establishes God's providential care that extends to all of humanity, encompassing both people and animals, restraining the forces of

Chapter 7 Exposing Satan's Use of Curses to Dethrone God

evil. It includes the Abrahamic Covenant, which holds the great promises that God has made to the Jewish people to establish Israel as the way to be blessed. The third covenant builds on the first two and is established through the life, death, and resurrection of Jesus Christ and provides the way of eternal salvation for all humanity.

The first of Satan's curses is embodied in the slogan, "**From the River to the Sea, Palestine will be Free.**" This is a direct assault on God's promise that He made to Abraham.

> On that day Adonai cut a covenant with Abram, saying, "I give this land to your seed, from the river of Egypt to the great river, the Euphrates River: the Kenite, the Kenizzites, the Kadmonites, the Hittites, the Perizzites, the Raphaites, the Amorites, the Canaanites, the Girgashites, and the Jebusites." Gen 15:18-21 TLV

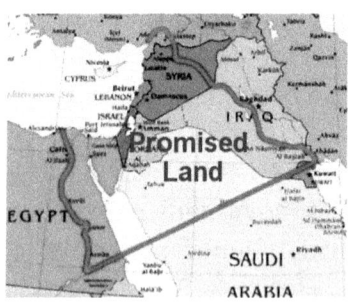

Alan Dershowitz draws out these implications and highlights the correlation with the Nazi agenda, which led to the Holocaust:

"Progressive students at many American universities issued statements, held banners, and participated in marches, not in favor of a two-state solution, which would establish a Palestinian state but rather against the existence of Israel. They were not pro-Palestinian; they were anti-Israel. The dominant slogan for these events was "Palestine will be free from the river to the sea." This wish is not ambiguous, for what it means is the ethnic cleansing of all Jewish Israelis from the land of Israel, including the parts of Israel that have been part of the nation-state of the Jewish people since its founding. It means a judenrein (free of Jews) Palestine, not a two-state solution, but a final solution for the Jews of Israel."[27]

---

[27] Pg. 74 Ibid. Dershowitz

What this means is destroying Israel as a Jewish state and killing all the Jews who inhabited these areas, which, of course, negates the promises that God has given Abraham.

Curses Negating the Prophetic Promises that the Jews Will Flourish in the Land, and that Jerusalem Will be the Throne of Adonai.

The second curse is embodied in all the calls for genocide of the Jews. This curse is most often camouflaged in clever slogans as well as projecting onto the Jews that they themselves have intentions of genocide toward Palestinians. Nevertheless, the intentions of this curse are stated by the demonic deception of Islam by those who have for decades chanted, "Death to America!" and "Death to Israel!" This curse of genocide is also being embodied in the recent permutations of Marxism, which is displayed in a multiplicity of movements that are standing in solidarity with Hamas and joining in with the cursing of Israel and the Jewish people.

The deep roots of this curse go back to the captivity in Egypt when Pharaoh decreed the death of male Hebrew children. This root was also manifested in the battle with the Amalekites seeking to block their way to the promised land and was demonstrated repeatedly in the attempts to exterminate the Jews as recorded in the Old Testament. These calls for genocide of the Jewish people were condoned in the Edict of Milan in 313, which did not extend protection of the Roman Empire and the Roman Catholic Church to born-again Jews.

Calls for persecution and genocide of the Jews have a long and terrible history by leaders of the Christian church. They were especially embodied in the writings of the great reformer, Martin Luther, who in later life was filled with hatred for the Jews which opened him up to becoming demonized. These curses, which Hitler used to deceive the German people and church, were written in Martin Luther's tract in 1543, *On the Jews and Their Lies* (*Von den Jüden und ihren Lügen*)

Chapter 7 Exposing Satan's Use of Curses to Dethrone God

These calls for genocide of the Jews have been voiced and acted upon for centuries and have been accompanied by a perverse "reversal and projection" strategy of Satan which was manifested at Harvard. [28]

The enemies of God are projecting their own stated intentions upon the Jews and upon Israel. This reversal and projection went so far as South Africa bringing allegations of genocide against Israel to the World Court in the Hague, while simultaneously excusing the actual intentions of genocide stated and implemented by Hamas. This is pointed out in Howard Jacobson's excellent article in The Guardian:

---

[28] The picture below, that focus on the supposed genocide of Palestinians is the theme of many pictures of protecters that may be found on the internet. This one pictured here come from the following: Pro-Palestinian, anti-Israel protesters gather at Harvard University, in Cambridge, Massachusetts, on October 14, 2023. (Joseph Prezioso / AFP) US congressional panel asks to see years of antisemitism complaints in Harvard probe | The Times of Israel

"Genocides don't leaflet the populations they want to destroy with warnings to stay out of harm's way, and Hamas, which Israel avowedly does want to see the back of, is not the Gazan people. For all the sensationalist pronouncements of academics who specialize in genocide, ethnic cleansing, apartheid, settler-colonialism, etc., the words simply flutter like so many pennants at a medieval joust. Denoting, in the fading light, which side you're on, no more. *The only party to a declared intention to commit genocide is Hamas...*" [29]

This projection works as a curse that draws deceived people into taking part in implementing Satan's plans for genocide of the Jewish people.

We can see this principle of projection at work in our everyday life, and that helps us understand how it works. When people have evil in their own hearts, they regard everyone around them as having the same evil motives and desires. If a man would like to cheat someone in a business deal, he will become convinced that that person is trying to cheat him and will see evidence of this even when it does not exist. In Psalm 69 David talks about how he is hated without cause and must repay what he did not steal. In Psalm 109 David says that his enemy love cursing "so it came to him."

Enforcing the Narrative of Jew-hatred Through Mob Violence

This strategy of projecting the curse of genocide away from

---

[29] *Charging Jews with genocide is to declare them guilty of precisely what was done to them – By Howard Jacobson, Sun 3 Dec 2023, "The only party to a declared intention to commit genocide is Hamas."*
https://www.theguardian.com/commentisfree/2023/dec/03/charging-jews-with-genocide-declare-them-guilty-precisely-what-was-done-to-them-middle-east

Chapter 7 Exposing Satan's Use of Curses to Dethrone God

Hamas and onto the Jews themselves has another chilling aspect to it. This narrative of Jew-hatred is being enforced through intimidation by mobs, bullying into silence anyone who supports Israel or holds opposing views. This characteristic is vividly documented by Caroline Glick on her show In-Focus, with the title: *From Seinfeld to Ben-Gvir, Antisemites Attack Jews:*[30]

> Jewish businesses or anybody who supports Israel in any way are being attacked across the world by far-left and Islamist mobs. Is this causing an awakening and a new realization about the nature of antisemitism?[31]

In this video she gives many examples of how these mobs are subverting and overturning the exercise of free speech, even to the point of impacting the parliamentary procedures which are the bedrock of our democratic processes. Especially damning are the reports of the British House of Commons, where long established procedures were changed because of threats and intimidation. What is taking place includes not just preparation for the destruction of Israel and extermination of the Jewish people, but also the destruction of our democratic societies. This is not new. It is a repeat of how, in the past, both Nazis, Communists and Islamists have snuffed out dissent and imposed their tyranny upon nation after nation.

These Calls for Genocide of Jews are Satan's Replacement of Judaism and Christianity through Islam and Marxism

---

[30] The Caroline Glick Show - YouTube
https://www.youtube.com/@thecarolineglickshow

[31] *From Seinfeld to Ben-Gvir, Antisemites Attack Jews*: February 27, 2024, by Caroline Glick, https://www.youtube.com/watch?v=QazmN_ch-TA

The root of this call for genocide of Jews by Muslims lies in the actions (the Sunna) and sayings (the Hadith) of Mohammad, who was supposed to be the model of the perfect man. In the Hadith he said:

> "Judgement Day will not come until the Muslims fight the Jews. The Jews will hide behind the stones and the trees, and the stones and the trees will say, oh Muslim, oh servant of Allah, there is a Jew hiding behind me — come and kill him."[32]

These calls for genocide of Jews are Satan's plans to counter the promises that God made to the Jewish people, promises which are presently being fulfilled with the growth of the Jewish population flourishing in the Land of Promise and with all nations gathering in Jerusalem as the "throne of Adonai."

> "It will be in those days when you multiply and become fruitful in the land." It is a declaration of Adonai. "They will no longer talk about the ark of the covenant of Adonai, nor will it come to mind or be remembered. Neither will it be missed or another one made again. At that time they will call Jerusalem the throne of Adonai and all the nations will gather into it, to Jerusalem, in the Name of Adonai. No longer will they walk according to the stubbornness of their evil heart. In those days the house of Judah will walk with the house of Israel. They will come together out of the land of the north to the land that I gave your fathers as an inheritance." (Jeremiah 3:16-18 TLV)

If the Jews living in the Land of Israel are all exterminated, then

---

[32] https://mydailykona.blogspot.com/2023/11/what-are-roots-of-israelipalestinian.html

how shall this promise of the blessings of multiplying and being fruitful be fulfilled? And further, if Jerusalem is destroyed and/or taken over by those who follow the manifestations of the spirit of the antichrist, how can it come to pass that Jerusalem will be called the "throne of Adonai?"

Satan's plans to Completely Replace God as Sovereign Lord by first exterminating the Jewish people.

Satan's plans, exposed and catalyzed in the October 7th Massacre, go much further than merely having a "Jew-free land of Israel." These calls for genocide of the Jewish people all through history, and now demonically energized by the atrocities against the Jews on October 7th, reveal the terrible depths of Satan's ultimate strategy. It is, essentially, to block the fulfillment of God's master plans for the "restoration of all things" through Jesus Christ, who brings the resurrection of the dead and the redemption of fallen humanity (Acts 3:21, Romans11:15). Satan's master plans are exposed to be as follows:

First, it is blocking the fulfillment of the Kingdom being restored to Israel, in which all nations will enter Jerusalem as the throne of Adonai.

Second, it is using all possible means in his formidable arsenal for blocking the fulfillment of the Great Commission. Jesus has stated that the Gospel of the Kingdom will be preached to all nations and then the end will come (Matthew 24:14). Satan is opposing this goal by whatever means are necessary, including the genocide of Jews and Christians, and even a catastrophic global war.

Third, and worst of all, it is abolishing God's covenants made with humanity by exterminating the very people with whom these covenants were made. Satan is seeking to dethrone God by destroying the covenant basis for God's work among humanity. Satan's plan is to condemn the human race to eternal death.

This raises the question of why anyone would want to destroy the state of Israel and call for the extermination of the Jewish people. Why would anyone even consider, much less make plans for, exterminating millions of innocent human beings?

I do not think the inspiration for the calls for the genocide of millions comes from people at all, but from the devil, who is the enemy of God and humanity.

This is not to excuse the people from being guilty of their terrible deeds. Rather, it is to point out that expressions of evil are a collaborative effort between Satan and those who have been deceived into his plans, willingly or otherwise. I believe the deep motive of both Satan and his human agents is found in their desire for absolute power. To accomplish this, they must dethrone God. Satan has already failed once to dethrone God in heaven, and so the strategy now is to dethrone Him by destroying God's Covenant people on earth.

But why would fellow human beings join with Satan in these terrible schemes? Let us look briefly into the abyss of evil in the era of the Holocaust and, with it, the capacity for humans to be deceived into being complicit in the evil by not believing it can exist.

How could Neville Chamberlain have gone to Munich in 1938 hoping to appease Adolf Hitler? Hitler had already demonstrated that he was not going to stop with just Czechoslovakia but had much greater plans. Chamberlain, who had seen so much suffering and destruction during the First World War, was a committed pacifist and could not believe that anyone would want war. But Hitler did.

As Hitler began persecuting the Jews of Germany the West (including the United States) generally closed their doors to any refugees – condemning many to their death. The attitude of the West was that, while things might be tough for Jews in Germany, they could not really be so bad.

Later, when the first reports of the Holocaust were presented to the world they were uniformly dismissed because even though Hitler had laid out explicitly what he wanted to do, none of the leaders of the West could bring themselves to believe that evil of that type existed. Instead, Western leaders claimed that all reports were "propaganda". This sat comfortably within their own

Chapter 7 Exposing Satan's Use of Curses to Dethrone God

experiences from World War One during which there had been very effective use of propaganda against the Germans, most of it fabricated. Jewish leaders had pleaded for the railroad lines going to the death camps to be bombed, but their pleas were ignored.

Only when stories were told and films were shown of the few survivors of the death camps and the piles of the dead did the West eventually believe what had been carefully documented long before that day. This came far too late for the survival of so many.

For my part I have struggled with these questions for a long time, ever since I was a ten year old boy! That is when I first saw ghastly pictures from the death camps and the Holocaust in Life Magazine. That was also when I read the book *Night* by Elie Wiesel.[33] It is the author's story of his experiences in the Nazi death camps, and he was about the same age as I was when I read his book. This book, described as a "Slim Volume of Terrifying Power," awakened in me an awareness of radical demonic evil and also, with it, a sense that somehow the Lord was calling me to have a role with Him in overcoming it.

Once, when I was in Israel, I met and spoke with the Messianic Jewish leader and teacher, Asher Intrater. I will never forget sitting in the offices of Tikkun near the Yad Hashmona overlooking the Judean hills where Jesus walked. I kept probing him with the questions that have always haunted me, "Why has there been the persistent call for the murder of the Jews? Why in the last hundred years has this been the call of Nazis, Radical Islam, and Marxists?" Asher's answer opened my eyes to aspects of the Bible that I had never appreciated from my non-Jewish, Gentile worldview. I have summarized our conversations by quoting from Asher's book *Who Ate Lunch With Abraham: The appearances of God in the form of a*

---

[33] This was published in 1960. I was born in 1951, and in the 1960s, there were still mass graves being discovered from the Nazi era. These were then pictured in Life Magazine. Actually, mass graves are still being located.
https://www.timesofisrael.com/not-forgotten-mass-graves-of-jewish-holocaust-victims-dedicated-in-poland/

Man in the Hebrew Scriptures.

Asher mentioned to me the three covenants that God has made with humanity:

> "There is a triangular covenant here. The New Covenant connects the forgiveness of sins to the preservation of natural creation. The creation of the world was made by covenant; the chosenness of the nation of Israel was made by covenant; and eternal salvation to all believers was made by covenant. These three are linked together by covenant."

Being Presbyterian, I was, of course, well-grounded in Covenant Theology as the way that the Sovereign God has decreed His relationship with humanity. But most of my focus had been on the New Covenant through Jesus Christ, coupled with the unbiblical tendency toward believing the New Covenant replaced the others. Those other covenants include the role of the Jewish people, the Land of Israel, the City of Jerusalem, and the expressions of God's common grace extended to all people, including the whole creation and the animal kingdom. Asher was helping me to understand all this better and to address these tendencies in my own thinking toward replacement theology. Then he said the following:

> "Covenant demands that either all three be true, or none of them. This is the secret spiritual root as to why both the Nazis and the Islamic Jihad set a goal to exterminate the Jewish people. If they had succeeded in destroying our people, then the New Covenant and the created order would have been in jeopardy.[34]

Frankly, this statement shook up my entire worldview! I have

---

[34] Intrater, Asher, *Who Ate Lunch With Abraham: The Appearances of God in the Form of a Man in the Hebrew Scriptures*. Frederick, MD: Revive Israel Media, 2011. Pg. 21. <www.reviveisrael.org>.

Chapter 7 Exposing Satan's Use of Curses to Dethrone God

pondered this deeply, and I believe it is true. This reveals God's way with His creation and humanity. It also exposes the actual depth of Satan's hatred and rebellion against God and God's people. Satan's plans are more audacious and sinister than merely replacing the faith of Jews and Christians with the deception of Islam, undermining the church of Jesus Christ with the anti-God ideologies of liberalism and Marxism, or taking measures to block the church from fulfilling Jesus' command, "He told them, "Go into all the world and proclaim the Good News to every creature." (Mark 16:15 TLV). Satan intends to replace God!

To achieve that goal, he is true to his nature as a murderer from the beginning. Satan, starting first with Jewish people and then extending his plans to include all those who have been engrafted into the Jewish root, is willing to murder millions, even billions, of human beings.[35] Replacing God by destroying the covenant basis of His relationship with humanity is the ultimate objective of Satan.

We have now identified the strategies of Satan and the rationale behind them. We are seeing the terrifying evidence that already, and in diverse ways, the winds of war and forebodings of calamity are upon us. It looks as though Satan's plans are gaining momentum and, unless soon stopped, will be moving toward their culmination, which has been envisioned in hell.

The urgent question is therefore: how is God, the Sovereign Lord of history, planning on stopping all this? How is He calling us to join Him in stopping this progression toward a geopolitical disaster. And how is He calling us to join in with His plans to restore the Kingdom to Israel and the fulfillment of the mission He has given us of taking the Gospel to all nations? We turn to this in the next chapter.

---

[35] Long, Brad, (Pg. 38-39 Prayer Strategy: For the Victory of Jesus Christ, by Zeb Bradford Long - PRMI Exousia Press)

Summary: Pointers for Praying

This is a spiritual battle where Satan's end goal is to replace God. To do that, he seeks to reverse the promises that God has made and the covenants (or agreements) that God has established with his people.

The primary way Satan seeks to achieve this is through curses. Here, his intentions are embodied in words and actions that can unleash demonic power to shape human hearts and attitudes so that the physical reality is established that promotes and advances Satan's vision.

While we're not called to engage with Satan directly, we can pray to affirm and proclaim the promises that God has made.

We can pray and affirm the covenantal promises of Scripture like Genesis 15:18-21 and Jeremiah 3:17.

- Lord, we thank you for giving this land to Israel.

- We thank you, Lord, for the promises you made to Abraham, Isaac, and Jacob about the Land of Israel.

- Adonai, thank you for your plans and purposes for Israel and the Jewish people.

- We praise you, Lord, that Jerusalem will be the throne of the Lord.

- We praise you that the nations will one day gather in Jerusalem to honor you.

- We thank you that you are a covenant-keeping God.

- We pray that you'll protect and establish your covenant promises.

- We praise you that those promises are Yes and Amen in Jesus Christ (2 Corinthians 1:20).

- We praise you that Jesus is the image of God and the firstborn of all creation (Colossians 1:15).

- We praise you that Christ is before all things, and in Him all things hold together (Colossians 1:17).

- We praise you that in Yeshua/Jesus, we are reconciled to God, no longer alienated from Him, but are adopted into sonship (Romans 8:15).

8
God's War Against Amalek

Let me briefly summarize what we have already covered. We have exposed how two expressions of the antichrist are joining together in their shared hatred of Jews, calling for the destruction of Israel and the extermination of the Jewish people. These have catalyzed the demonic movements that are already at work on earth to lead to the possibility, not only of genocide of Jews, but also of a conflagration that could engulf the world in a catastrophic war.

I believe the Oct 7th Massacre and the resulting Israel/Hamas war was the decisive tipping point at which God's judgment or blessings of the peoples and nations was taking place. Within the spiritual and human realms, a division occurred between nations, movements, and individuals. The deep source of this division is based on God's plumbline as stated in Genesis 12:1-3 – God's judgments and blessings are determined by whether one participates in blessing or in cursing the Jewish people and those grafted into them through faith in Jesus Christ. The ultimate blessing of eternal salvation is received by the way of salvation through the Jewish people, culminating in Yeshua (Jesus), who has come as their Messiah.

> This Yeshua is 'the stone—rejected by you, the builders—that has become the chief cornerstone.' There

is salvation in no one else, for there is no other name under heaven given to mankind by which we must be saved!" (Act 4:11-12 TLV)

The Sovereign God has established this basis of blessing and cursing, which it and results in both a temporal and an eternal alignment among nations, political movements, and individuals. In our epoch, the decisive question becomes: Are they taking part in blessing Israel and the Jewish people, or are they siding with and supporting those who would curse Israel with destruction and call for the genocide of the Jewish people?

This division has reverberations worldwide and is exacerbating the many divisions and hotspots on Earth, any one of which could ignite a global war which could even go nuclear. Frankly, our situation looks rather desperate! For those with a historical perspective, current events seem like a deja vu of the nightmare of the 1930s when Jew-hatred went viral and unchecked! So how does all this stop? How do we prevent this evil from metastasizing and sending the world into an abyss?

What is the Sovereign God Doing about those who are cursing Israel?

We may look at the state of the world with alarm and be stirred to take action in a desire to prevent this impending disaster. However, we must rid ourselves of any pretention that we can prevent this on our own. This is God's issue! The Lord is the one who has set the criteria for judging the nations in His promise to Abraham. It is He, not us, who will implement His blessings and curses.

These are His people - the Jews and those who have been grafted into them by faith in Jesus Christ - who are being threatened with genocide. These are His plans to "restore the Kingdom to Israel." His plan for "the preaching the Gospel of the Kingdom to all nations," leading to the "restoration of all things," will all be disastrously delayed if Satan even partially succeeds in his vile schemes. So, we cry out, "Lord, what are you doing about all this?" I believe the Lord has given us clear and decisive answers to this question in His Word.

The first is the Old Testament example of the Battle with Amalek recorded in Exodus 17.

> "Remember what Amalek did to you along the way as you came out from Egypt—how he happened upon you along the way and attacked those among you in the rear, all the stragglers behind you, when you were tired and weary—he did not fear God." (Deuteronomy 25:17-18 TLV)

If this attack had been successful, it could have prevented them from making their rendezvous with God on Mt. Sinai, thereby thwarting God's salvation plans for all people through the Jewish people.

The Lord clearly reveals His strategies for defeating His enemies who are cursing His people and blocking His kingdom plans.

God Declared a Just War on Amalek For All Generations

The outlines of the battle in Exodus 17:8-16 TLV are as follows:

> Then the Amalekites came and fought with Israel at Rephidim. (9) Moses said to Joshua, "Choose men, go out, and fight the Amalekites. Tomorrow I will stand on the top of the hill with the staff of God in my hand." (10) So Joshua did as Moses said, and fought the Amalekites, while Moses, Aaron and Hur went up to the top of the hill. (11) When Moses held up his hand, Israel prevailed. But when he let down his hand, the Amalekites prevailed. (12) Moses' hands grew heavy, so they took a

Chapter 8 God's War Against Amalek

stone, put it under him, and he sat down. Aaron and Hur held up his hands, one on each side. So his hands were steady until the sun went down. (13) So Joshua overpowered the Amalekites and his army with the edge of the sword. (14) Adonai said to Moses, "Write this for a memorial in the book, and rehearse it in the hearing of Joshua, for I will utterly blot out the memory of the Amalekites from under heaven." (15) Then Moses built an altar, and called the name of it Adonai-Nissi. (16) Then he said, "By the hand upon the throne of Adonai, Adonai will have war with Amalek from generation to generation."

Who are the Amalekites: Then and Now?

The Amalekites were the descendants of Esau's son, Eliphaz, by the concubine Timna, who gave birth to Amalek (Genesis 36:11-12). According to Deuteronomy 25:17-19, they were a marauding band who attacked the Hebrews when they were most vulnerable during their journey out of Egypt. The Amalekites tried to block the Israelites on their way to the promised land, and Israel had to battle against them several more times during their early history.

In 1 Samuel 15, we have the story of Samuel, the prophet who anointed Saul as King and ordered him to fulfill God's command to wipe out the Amalekites. This chapter reports on the battle, noting that Saul did not fully accomplish what the Lord had ordered because he allowed King Agag of Amalek to live, as well as the best of the animals. Because of this disobedience, King Saul lost his kingdom, and his successor, King David, also had to fight these same descendants of Amalek. Who were these people against whom God had declared war for all generations?

It is noted that Amalek *"did not fear God."* This is the key to understanding who Amalek was then - a people group who did not fear God. They were opposed to God and God's people. The fact that they did not "fear God" means that they had therefore opened themselves up to the devil, who is opposed to God. I believe that

God's declaration that He would be at war with Amalek from generation to generation suggests that Amalek is also symbolic of Satan and the demons under his thrall, who are committed to blocking God from accomplishing His kingdom purposes on earth through His chosen people. These demonic powers have always expressed Satan's hatred and rebellion against God and God's people through the agency of those who "do not fear God" and have thus been deceived into carrying out Satan's plans by their hatred, first of God's people, the Jews, and then of God Himself.

There has been a long, bloody history of those who have embodied the demonic spirit of Amalek and have hated and conceived evil against the Jews. This has involved a great host, including Mohammad and many of those who have followed him. Tragically, this includes the great reformer, Martin Luther who, in later life, was filled with a virulent hatred of the Jews and called for their persecution. Karl Marx, though Jewish, was filled with hatred, not just of Jews but of humanity, leading to mass death and suffering wherever his ideas were imposed. Adolf Hitler's hatred of the Jews infected a whole nation and led them to participate in genocide. This has manifested most recently through Hamas, the Islamic Republic of Iran, BLM, the United Nations, and others who have given themselves over to hatred of the Jews, calling for their destruction – even through the naïve college students who are parroting the Islamic desire to claim Israel's promised land, "Palestine will be free from the River to the Sea."

The role of the United Nations in this is especially troubling. There is now evidence exposing what has long been suspected that some agencies of the UN have been subverted by malevolent powers and become demonic strongholds both enabling and actually implementing the curse of genocide against the Jews. It turns out that there is indisputable proof that hundreds of the employees of UNRWA (The United Nations Relief and Works Agency for Palestine Refugees in the Near East) took part in the slaughter and torture of Jewish men women and children including babies October 7th. In a January 30th, 2024, article in the Times of Israel this is reported: "Blinken says evidence of UNRWA staffers'

Chapter 8 God's War Against Amalek

Oct. 7 involvement 'highly, highly credible'"[36] This is further confirmed by all the other evidence that is coming out as the IDF have made progress in destroying the Hamas tunnel network killing Hamas operatives and gathering troves of intelligence. They even found right under the UNRWA headquarters in Gaza City a network of Hamas tunnels as well as a major computer data centers. Of course, the UN claims to know nothing about this but the facts shows otherwise.[37] All this undisputable evidence against the UN agency has led to the inescapable conclusion that, "UNRWA is Hamas!"[38] Is that not enough evidence to demonstrate that UNRWA and with it the United Nations is among the vanguard members or the coalition of Amalekites implementing this curse of genocide against the Jewish people?

God has stated that He is at war with the Amalekites of each generation – those who have, whether willingly or through being deceived, entered into Satan's plans to destroy the Jewish people and thereby block the gospel of the Kingdom going to all nations.

In the October 7th attack, we see this high-level Satanic power fully at work embodying the devil's plans (the destruction of Israel

---

[36] *Blinken says evidence of UNRWA staffers' Oct. 7 involvement 'highly, highly credible' –News outlets publish photos of UN staffers implicated in Israeli dossier; New Zealand pauses funding over 'incredibly serious allegations; Israel cancels meetings with UNRWA head,* https://www.timesofisrael.com/blinken-says-evidence-of-unrwa-staffers-oct-7-involvement-highly-highly-credible/

[37] *Directly beneath UNRWA's Gaza headquarters, IDF uncovers top secret Hamas data center: Subterranean facility for terror group's intelligence needs, beneath UN complex in upscale Rimal neighborhood, discovered after interrogations of Palestinian prisoners By EMANUEL FABIAN 10 February 2024,* https://www.timesofisrael.com/directly-beneath-unrwas-gaza-headquarters-idf-uncovers-top-secret-hamas-data-center/

[38] *SHOCKING: New Evidence Proves UNRWA Is Hamas | The Caroline Glick Show In-Focus, Mar 5, 2024,* https://www.youtube.com/watch?v=lEF5Yjq-Pug

and the extermination of the Jewish people) against God's plans. Hamas was established in 1988, and its founding charter established its DNA – its core character. This charter calls for the destruction of Israel and the killing of Jews. Article 7 of that founding charter provides what they consider to be a divine sanction for their goals and the atrocities they committed by citing this Hadith: "The Day of Judgment will not come about until Muslims fight Jews and kill them. Then, the Jews will hide behind rocks and trees, and the rocks and trees will cry out: 'O Muslim, there is a Jew hiding behind me, come and kill him."[39]

So, the October 7th Massacre is a clear expression of the heart of Islamic Jihadist Hamas, proving they do not fear the God of Abraham, Isaac and Jacob, and proving themselves to be the embodiment of the high-level demonic spirit of Amalek in this epoch.

God has declared in this war that "...I will utterly blot out the memory of the Amalekites from under heaven." This is a severe statement that I believe has both temporal and spiritual implications.

The temporal manifestation is found in the reality that God has declared war against the Amalekites and ordered His people in Bible times to utterly destroy them in military actions. Because of the disobedience of God's people in Bible history the Amalekites, as a group of people, were not wiped out. The result was that they continued to give problems to Israel. But why would a loving God announce, "I will utterly blot out the memory of the Amalekites from under heaven." I think the reason, in the Old Testament as well as in the case of contemporary Amalekites like Hamas and the Iranian Ayatollahs, is that they have intentionally and publicly

---

[39] (From https://americanmilitarynews.com/2021/05/hamas-terror-groups-charter-explicitly-calls-for-israels-destruction-fight-jews-and-kill-them/)

announced their intentions of exterminating the Jewish people, beginning in Israel.

If Israel is to survive and the Jewish people are to continue to be a means of God's blessings for the nations, there is no other option than for God to blot out the memory from under heaven of these enemies of the Jews, unless they repent of this hideous goal. In this present war with Hamas, that is precisely what Prime Minister Netanyahu has promised to do. Until Hamas repents from these stated goals, what other realistic options are there?

This state of war that God has declared in our generation against Amalek also extends to all the others who are cursing Israel. This includes Iran and its proxies the Houthis of Yemen and Hezbollah in Lebanon, the nations who are aligning with Hamas, radical left Marxist movements like BLM including even those students naively caught up in these movements, politicians and members of governments especially in the United States, United Kingdom and Canada. Those nations based on biblical Judeo-Christian values will be held especially culpable because their joining in cursing of Israel represents an abandonment of their foundations which have been the basis of God's past blessings poured out upon them.

The call upon all of those who are participating in this cursing of Israel in these diverse ways is to repent! Repent! While there is still time and before they bring themselves under the curse. And if they do not, God's war against them will work itself out according to His sovereign plans. Not all of course will be defeated through bloody military conflict, but there are many ways that God's blessings will be withheld with in the human and material realms. This will depend on the context they are in. For instance, in the United States politicians may be voted out of office or their evil constrained by other branches of Government. For those students involved in these woke movements, there is the urgent need for them to hear the gospel of Jesus Christ and be brought into God's kingdom, where they may be set free from their anti-biblical Judeo-Chritian worldviews.

For sure the spiritual consequence when people do not fear God and reject and seek to destroy the way of salvation established through the Jewish people and the Messiah, Yeshua, is that they condemn themselves to eternal death.[40] The gospel of John declares,

> "Now this is the judgment, that the light has come into the world and men loved the darkness instead of the light, because their deeds were evil. For everyone who does evil hates the light and does not come to the light, so that their deeds will not be exposed. But whoever practices the truth comes to the light, so that it may be made known that his deeds have been accomplished in God." (John 3:19-21 TLV)

In this war, God will judge such actions, and those who took the roles of the Amalekites will be blotted out from under heaven. Ultimately this will take place on the Day of Judgment, when those who have taken the role of the Amalekites in their generation and have not repented from it will have their names removed from the Book of Life.

While I'm sure that God is faithful to His Word and will wage this war to the end, I am equally convinced that God is loving and just and, as it says in 2 Peter 3:9, "He is being patient toward you—not wanting anyone to perish, but for all to come to repentance." Therefore, our priority as intercessors is to pray that those who are committed to carrying out the plans for the genocide of the Jewish people will, instead, repent and be brought to saving faith in Jesus Christ. However, our prayers may also be for God to carry out His just judgment and remove these people who do not fear Him and are committed to their genocidal ambitions. We must be ready to be led by the Holy Spirit to know when it is time to shift from

---

[40] I know this is a harsh statement, but it is based on the clear affirmations of the Holy Spirit i.e. Acts 4:11-12. I believe however that there is room within the vastness of God's love, mercy and grace, for those whom Paul identified as "those who fear God and keep God's law which is written in their heart even though they do not know the law." Romans 2:12-16

Chapter 8 God's War Against Amalek

praying for them to repent and, instead, to pray for their removal before they can do further damage.

Two Biblical Models Revealing the Lord's Strategy for Defeating Amalek

The Strategy of Moses as Intercessor and Joshua as Warrior

The way that the Lord God chose to fight His first battle with Amalek provides us with a model that we may also be called to emulate.

In this first battle, the Lord revealed to Moses the following strategy: Moses said to Joshua, "Choose men, go out, and fight the Amalekites. Tomorrow, I will stand on the top of the hill with the staff of God in my hand." [41]

This approach was necessary because the battle was against those people who did not fear God – the Amalekites, who were armed with physical weapons. It was also against the powers and principalities who were working through these people. The dual nature of the conflict required a unique battle strategy. Today, God's war against Hamas is with the human armies, armed with weapons of death, as well as with the demons in the people and those behind them who are manifesting Satan's power of death.

There is another observation to make from this story of the battle between the Israelites and the Amalekites. We find that there is a complex interrelationship between God working in the intercessor and God working in those who are working in physical actions to do his will. Through this complex relationship, we see God's Kingdom work taking place.

---

[41] ***Victory O Lord!*** is an 1871 painting by John Everett Millais depicting Moses, Aaron and Hur during the Battle of Rephidim against the Amalekites. This Photo by Unknown Author is licensed under CC BY-SA

Breaking the Curse of Genocide against the Jews

Moses is up on the hill interceding; Joshua is fighting in the valley. Notice the connection between prayer and physical action; Moses is obedient in prayer, and Joshua is obedient through his actions as he leads the army into battle. If either stopped doing what they were called to do, the battle would be lost.

It is important to note that neither Moses nor Joshua worked alone. Moses was backed up by Aaron and Hur, who held up his hands. An army of warriors accompanied Joshua. This teaches us that while there might be prominent leaders, these roles may also be corporate, with many supporting roles.

Today, God has chosen to wage war against those who embody Amalek in the same way that He did in the battle described in Exodus 17. God's method of defeating the attack on Israel and the threats of genocide against the Jewish people is the same today as then. There must be a dynamic combination of intercession and spiritual warfare on the one hand, and on the other hand the application of all the instruments of national power, including military force, to defeat the present manifestations of Amalek. This is necessary because the enemy is both demonic and human.

God is calling into His service those who will be in the roles of Moses (with Aaron and Hur) to do the work of intercession and spiritual warfare. He is also calling those like Joshua and his army who work to defeat the array of human movements that are attacking Israel and are working to implement genocide of the Jewish people. There will be multiple dimensions in both coordinated forms of God's means for waging war. For instance,

Chapter 8 God's War Against Amalek

the spiritual battle will include engaging with different levels of demonic beings. These include demons that are deceiving and/or possessing individual Jihadists, but also the higher-level demons possessing their leaders, and the highest level of demons who are not attached to people at all but directing the human and spiritual war from the heavenly realms. The battlefield in the human realm will include not only the actual firefights between armed groups, but also the political, ideological and communication spheres. The "Joshuas" here will consist not only of soldiers, but also politicians, news commentators, and a host of others.[42]

In this great battle of this present generation, all of us will have a role. Frankly, it is little different from the great battles that my parents' generation fought in overcoming the embodiment of Amalek in the Nazis in the great conflicts of the 1930s to 1945, and again later in the protracted war with the manifestation of Amalek that was embodied in the antichrist ideology of Soviet and Chinese Marxist/Leninism. God's war against Amalek continues in all its present-day manifestations. In our present era, the Lord Yeshua (Jesus), the commander of the Lord's armies, calls up the "Joshua workers" and the "Moses workers" to be deployed within every dimension of reality: the church, society and government, nationally and internationally.

This book is directed primarily toward all those whom God called into the spiritual battle as intercessors, spiritual warriors, and frontline witnesses to Jesus Christ - those called into the roles of Moses, Aaron, and Hur. In the chapters that follow, we will be introducing practical strategies for intercession and spiritual warfare that we believe the Holy Spirit is calling us to deploy right now in order to block Satan's plans of destroying Israel and exterminating the Jewish people. We will leave the commentary on the war strategies and geopolitical dynamics to others. However, we must never forget that these two dimensions are

---

[42] In PRMI's Advanced course on Strategic Level Intercession and Spiritual Warfare we provide a much more in-depth teaching on this topic, especially on the different battle spaces which require different strategies and tactics.

interconnected. We must recognize that the way our prayers will be answered is often through politicians, government leaders, military personnel, cultural leaders, the media, and the social structures. As long we live in a fallen world and, as long as God's and Satan's works are mediated through individuals and social structures, there will always be a political aspect to this work of intercession. So, we must consider all this as we are called up the mountain as intercessors. Indeed, it has been my experience that if the Holy Spirit is leading us then, while we may be operating from our position seated with Jesus Christ in the heavenly places, we will not be absent from bloody military confrontations on the battlefields, or from the geopolitical clashes taking place, or from the local and national political battles, in which there will be conflicting opinions. Indeed, we may find ourselves called right into the thick of them. However, those called as intercessors will not be dealing directly with human enemies but with the supernatural powers of darkness. For this, we will need to put on the full armor of God, for our battle will be with the devil and the high-level demons who are behind human operations.

Though we will be called to transcend politics, we will still be faced with the terrible necessity of taking part in God's war with the modern expressions of Amalek, and this will lead us not to a state of detached neutrality but rather to total involvement in these terrible struggles. We will be called to work with God as He blesses those who bless Israel and comes against those who curse Israel. Our role will include praying for God to raise up those government leaders who will bless Israel and oppose those implementing the curse of genocide. This involves praying that the Lord will remove those taking part in cursing Israel. For those intercessors living in democratic societies the Lord will often call us to embody our faith through voting and other actions appropriate for advancing God's Kingdom through government and society. However, from our "place of intercession," we will be called to transcend politics and military clashes, and this will put us in the position of being the means that God the Father uses to shape His agenda in and through human events. [43]

The Jews Defeating Haman the Amalekite's Curse of Genocide

Let us turn now to another manifestation of the Amalekites, which was embodied in Haman unleashing the curse of genocide against the Jewish People. This is recorded in the book of Esther and tells the story of how Queen Esther was used by God to reverse the curse of genocide against the Jews who, at that time, were a vulnerable minority scattered in different cities in the Persian Empire, which was based in modern day Iran. This took place between 470 to 460 BC during the Exile. We need not go into the whole story, which is a quick read. However, the following observations are relevant for understanding God's present war with Amalek.

First, is the observation that God has announced that He is at war with Amalek from generation from generation. The particular spiritual and human manifestation of Amalek seeking the extermination of the Jews, in Queen Esther's era was Haman who was, in fact, a direct descendant of Agag king of the Amalekites. Haman is enraged that Mordecai does not bow down to him and honor him in his position above everyone else. To get revenge Haman builds a gallows 75 feet high just for Mordecai. However, when Haman realizes that Mordecai is Jewish, his rage moves from arranging the murder of one man, to plotting the murder of a whole people, which is genocide. With ten thousand talents of silver Haman was able to bribe and deceive the King into his diabolical schemes. The result was that:

> "The king took his signet ring from his hand and gave it to Haman—son of Hammedatha the Agagite—enemy of the Jews. The king said to Haman, "The silver and the

---

[43] I have written about this dilemma of being an intercessor who transcend Politics and yet intensely involved in my book, *Called Beyond Politics into History Shaping Prayer*.

people are yours—do with them as you please"'" (Est 3:10-11 TLV)

So the edict was made in the kings name, launching the curse of genocide.

> Dispatches were sent by couriers into all the king's provinces, stating to destroy, slay, and annihilate all the Jews—from the youth to the elderly, both little children and women—on a single day, the thirteenth day of the twelfth month, the month of Adar, and to plunder their possessions. Est 3:13 TLV

Why did Haman's need for revenge move from destroying just one man to destroying an entire race of people? Would not have hanging Mordecai on a 75-foot gallows been enough to satisfy this man's wounded pride? This genocidal extension to all Jews suggests that there were more than human forces at work. Could it be that a high-level demon of death to the Jews had passed down the generations from the first Amalekites, and was now welcomed to take control because of Haman's anger and hatred towards Mordecai? The result was the satanic curse of genocide was being manifested through him. Jew-hatred – whether in Haman, Hitler, Hamas, or whoever – opens the doors to demonic deception and even possession, and this paves the way for the control of Satan who is a "murderer from the beginning", especially of God's chosen people. There are chilling parallels today in Iran (formerly Persia), with the Ayatollah echoing Haman's efforts by calling for Israel's destruction on numerous occasions.

Second, we must explore just how God waged war against Haman and those who were ready to join in fulfilling this curse of genocide that been unleashed upon the Jewish people. Now we come to a very interesting observation: This is essentially the same strategy that God deployed in the first battle with the Amalekites. In that battle the emphasis is on the role of Moses the Intercessor, with Joshua and the army in the background. Now in the book of

Chapter 8 God's War Against Amalek

Esther the emphasis has shifted to the Joshuas empowered to fight the battle.

The role of intercession is not overtly named but is included in the repeated references that at each phase of the unfolding events there is a call to fasting. While God is never mentioned in the entire book of Esther, fasting is the way of invoking God's help in the time of crisis.

We see this when Queen Esther hearkens to Mordecai's planned attack and decides to break the law by entering into the King's presence without being summoned. In a tacit acknowledgment that this will take Divine assistance she makes the following request:

> "Go! Gather together all the Jews who are in Shushan and fast for me. Do not eat or drink for three days, night or day. My maids and I will fast in the same way. Afterwards, I will go in to the king, even though it is not according to the law. So if I perish, I perish!" Est 4:16 TLV

She finds favor with the King, setting in motion a series of events which lead to the reversal of the curse of genocide against the Jews. First, Haman - the one who implemented Satan's scheme - found himself hanging from the gallows that he had prepared for Mordecai, with all his possessions given to Esther the Jew!

Second to deal with the army of Amalekites who had been summoned to carry out the curse, by killing all the Jews and stealing their property, the King who could not undo his own edict made another decree:

> The king granted the right for Jews in every city to assemble themselves and to protect themselves—to destroy, kill and annihilate any army of any people or province that might attack them and their women and children, and to plunder their possessions. (Est 8:11 TLV)

In other words, the way the curse of genocide was undone was that the Jews themselves were empowered by the human authority and by Divine authority, to take up arms and destroy their own enemies. This is described in the following:

> Jews assembled in their cities throughout all the provinces of King Ahasuerus in order to lay hands on those seeking their harm. No one was able to stand against them, for fear of them had fallen on all the peoples. Even all the administrators of the provinces, the officers and governors, and those doing business for the king, helped the Jews, for the dread of Mordecai had fallen on them. Mordecai was prominent at the palace, and his fame spread throughout all the provinces. The man Mordecai was growing ever more powerful. The Jews struck down all their enemies with the sword, killing and destroying, and they did whatever they wished to those who hated them. (Est 9:2-5 TLV)

Notice the way that the Jews had divine favor in that the fear of them fell upon all who ended up helping them. And further note that this was not a campaign of extermination against everyone who was not Jewish but only against those who had attacked them. The casualties of those killed by the Jews are listed as follows:

"In the citadel at Shushan the Jews killed and destroyed 500 people," "they killed 300 men in Shushan," (Esther 9:6,15):

The summary the number of casualties from the whole campaign is reported as follows:

> Meanwhile the rest of the Jews who were in the king's provinces gathered together to protect themselves and to get relief from their enemies. They killed 75,000 of their enemies, but they did not lay their hands on the plunder. (Est 9:16 TLV)

By the listing of the exact and limited numbers of people killed in each city, it is made clear that this was not a rampage of carnage and death against innocent people. Notice something else about this phase of God's war against the Amalekites. It is noted several times that the victorious Jews, "did not lay their hands on the plunder." This demonstrates that the counter attacks were not motivated by financial gain but for self-defense. While there were a lot of casualties and no doubt some innocent people were included as collateral damage, however this was not genocide, but Divine justice meted out to those who had planned the extermination of the Jews.

Applying the Lessons to Our Present Epoch

First, the right to self-defense is among those inalienable rights that I believe God has given to all people made in his image. This is built into the American Constitution and is the basis for the Second Amendment which is the right to be armed. But this right is based on the Noahic Covenant (Genesis 8:20-9:17) given to all humankind and includes the animal kingdom. It is also based on the Ten Commandments given to the Jewish people and all those engrafted into them through faith in Yeshua. Murder is forbidden because we are made in God's image. If one does murder, then there is the divine right for the person who committed the murder to in turn be killed.

> Surely your lifeblood will I avenge. From every animal and from every person will I avenge it. From every person's brother will I avenge that person's life. The one who sheds human blood, by a human will his blood be shed, for in God's image He made humanity. (Gen 9:5-6 TLV)

Now this, as Abraham Kuyper so aptly points out, is not a warrant for individuals to go get revenge, which just leads to lawlessness and more death. Instead, this is the basis for the institution of government authority.[44] Now let's apply all of this to our present situation and to the unleashing of the curse of genocide of Jews that took place in the October 7th Hamas massacre.

In the days of Queen Esther, the Jews were a minority people, in the Persian Empire. They really had no way to defend themselves either from the majority of people or from the government authorities. So, when the decree went out to exterminate them, they were really helpless. This sentence of certain death could not be commuted. But through the intervention of Queen Esther, no doubt aided by divine wisdom, the King made another decree. The Jews were delegated the right by the King himself, who in effect was the government, to implement the requirement of the Noahic covenant, that the one who sheds human blood must in turn be killed. Except this divinely required justice was carried out as a preemptive attack by the Jews themselves to prevent their own extermination.

Now in our epoch, unlike that of the Jews in the Persian Empire, and many other world empires, God has raised up the state of Israel as a sovereign nation. Israel as a nation has the God-given right of self-defense and the obligation to protect its own citizens. So now the way that God has decided to wage war against those Amaleks seeking the destruction of the Jews is through the nation state of Israel.

Is it not indicative that this right of a sovereign nation to defend itself is accepted for every nation on earth, but is constantly questioned about the state of Israel? This goes even further, does this question whether Israel even has the right to exist at all? No one questions the right for the sovereign nation of Jordan to exist or to defend itself. Yet this nation was created by the very same international mandates and treaties that created the state of Israel. The establishment of the State of Israel is actually on firmer ground

---

[44] Kuyper, Abraham Common Grace: God's Gifts For a Fallen World, Volume 1: The Historical Section, Acton Institute, Lexham Press, Bellingham WA. 2016. Pgs. 74-82

Chapter 8 God's War Against Amalek

then the creation of any of the surrounding states, in that it honored the actual 3000 years history of the Jewish people in the Land. Is this not a case of Satan setting up the circumstances in which the curse of genocide may be implemented against Israel and the Jewish people?

Israel as a sovereign state has not only the right to defend itself and protect itself against its enemies who have not only recently spoken of the curse of genocide of the Jews but have taken measures to implement it. This is just what Israel is doing in its present war with Hamas and must also do against their other enemies who are dedicated to their destruction, like Iran. Israel's right to self-defense and God's call to those intercessors, movements, and nations, who are called to join with the Jews in God's war against the gathered armies of Amalek, is however not license for genocide of an entire race of people. It is rather a just war against those who have themselves joined in implementing the curse of genocide. A war in which there will be many innocent people killed especially with Hamas' tactics of embedding itself in and under a civilian population to use them as human shields.

Now Israel, being a small nation, cannot accomplish this on their own, they need the support of other nations. It is at this point that we must see past all the geopolitics and big power politics into the working out of God's plans. He is dividing individuals, peoples, movements, nations, and transnational movements, according to those who either bless or curse Israel. Those who bless Israel are those who will be allied with Israel in providing the military, financial, moral means for Israel to push back and defend itself against those nations and powers that are seeking her destruction. This is just what is taking place now. How all this is working out with many being deceived by the narrative of the Jew-Haters, is up in the air and in doubt and we are at an extremely dangerous tipping point.

God's War against Iranian Ayatollahs

There is one implication from what we learned from the Book of

Esther that has a direct spiritual connection to our present situation in which the Islamic Republic of Iran—a modern successor of the biblical Persian Empire, is the most powerful embodiment of Amalek. I would contend that its leadership demonstrate through their virulent hatred of Israel and the Jews and their Fatwahs calling for the total annihilation of Israel and Jews worldwide that they are influenced, or even possessed, by the same high-level demons who possessed Haman, Adolph Hitler and the leaders of Hamas.

I would further contend the true source of the curse of genocide that is being enacted through Iran's proxies' Hamas, Hezbollah and others, is from the Ayatollahs themselves. Granted that this curse is received by Hamas and others, and resonates with their hatred and goals, but it is linked to this higher source.

Let us trace back, the curse of genocide against the Jews that go back to Persia. Notice that the edict made by the King in book of Esther setting in motion the curse of genocide of the Jews was not broken or repented of, but its effects were just diminished or prevented at that time, by the same King restoring the divine right of the Jews to defend themselves. This curse was also no doubt ameliorated again by the actions of Cyrus the Great in blessing Israel. However, in the spiritual realm the curse remains: "… destroy, slay, and annihilate all the Jews—from the youth to the elderly, both little children and women—on a single day, the thirteenth day of the twelfth month, the month of Adar, and to plunder their possessions," (Esther 3:13). Down through the centuries Satan has adapted and, again and again, unleashed this curse of genocide against the Jews. This has taken different forms in different ages, and with different embodiments of Amalek. A recent iteration of the curse behind present events was made by Iran's supreme leader Ayatollah Ali Khamenei in 2012. This was reported in an article entitled: "Ayatollah: Kill All Jews, Annihilate Israel": Iran lays out their legal case for a genocidal attack against a 'cancerous tumor.'

> The Iranian government, through a website proxy, has laid out the legal and religious justification for the

destruction of Israel and the slaughter of its people. The doctrine includes wiping out Israeli assets and Jewish people worldwide. Calling Israel a danger to Islam, the conservative website alif, with its ties to Iran's supreme leader, Ayatollah Ali Khamenei, said the opportunity must not be lost to remove "this corrupting material. It is a 'jurisprudential justification' to kill all the Jews and annihilate Israel, and in that, the Islamic government of Iran must take the help." [45]

Notice the roundabout way that this word was spoken, suggestive of demonic cloaking. This came from a proxy web site with its ties to the supreme leader. Regardless of whether the words are spoken directly by the supreme leader or released by a proxy, they come with the imprimatur of the supreme leader. As an Ayatollah, which means "sign of Allah", these words have the definite sanction of Allah and are backed up by the "jurisprudential justification," which means confirmed by the sacred texts of Islam. This is a modern day restatement of Haman's curse of genocide against the Jewish people, a curse which is amplified by the ritualistic chanting of "Death to Israel" and "Death to America" by Muslim mobs every Quds Day (Jerusalem Day) since 1979.[46]

This curse was unleashed by the supreme leaders in 2012 at a time of heightened expectation that the 12th Imam was about to return. This was a time of great danger for Israel and the world

---

[45] Reza Kahlili, "Ayatollah: Kill All Jews, Annihilate Israel," Feb. 5 2012, World Net Daily, http://www.wnd.com/2012/02/ayatollah-kill-all-jews-annihilate-israel/

[46] **Chanting 'Death to Israel,' tens of thousands march in Tehran for 'Jerusalem Day'** Senior officials, including President Raisi, attend central rally in capital, which comes amid deadly violence in Israel and warning of looming war with Iran, By AGENCIES and TOI STAFF 14 April 2023, https://www.timesofisrael.com/chanting-death-to-israel-tens-of-thousands-march-in-tehran-for-jerusalem-day/

because of the apocalyptic belief that the 12th Imam's return would be hastened by such actions as attacking Israel. In preparing for the return, the Ayatollah had announced that Iran must lead the way.

With a team of other intercessors, I was called into the heavenlies into major prayer battles to block the fulfillment of this curse. I believe it was for a season. [47] However, this curse has never been rescinded or overturned by Iran by choosing to bless rather than curse Israel. This curse has now been reembodied, reinvigorated and unleased in the October 7th Massacre. It is now bearing its bitter fruit of stirring Jew-hatred worldwide and catalyzing an alignment of movements and nations against Israel. Israel.

This present-day embodiment of the armies of Amalek carrying out the curse of genocide of against the Jews will not be fully broken simply with Hamas either renouncing their charter or being totally destroyed. It needs the Ayatollahs themselves to turn from cursing Israel to blessing Israel. We must pray that this happens both in the spiritual as well as human realms before God's war against Amalek escalates to include them as well. Finally, the model of how God chose to wage war in Esther's day, may at some point need to be implemented, which is preemptive war against those who are seeking to exterminate the Jewish people before they can carry out their deadly plans. In all this our role as the Church of Jesus Christ and as intercessors, if we are to be in alignment with God's promises of blessing, will be to stand with the Jews as they exercise their God given right of self-defense through the means the Lord has provided which is the sovereign state of Israel.

Our ultimate objective is praying that the curse of genocide will not only be countered, but entirely revoked. This can only happen

---

[47] I give the background and the results of this strategic level prayer battle in my book, *Prayer Strategy –For the Victory of Jesus Christ: Book II Defeating Demonic Strongholds of ISIS and Radical Islam*, PRMI Exousia Press 2016. Pg. 185- 187. The entire chapter 12 about breaking curses from Islam is relevant to our role in God's war against the present manifestation of Amalek in Hamas.

through the blood of the Jewish Messiah on the Cross.

Preparation before Moving into this Next Phase

Before embarking upon this assignment, I need to warn of some dangers. Usually, this work of high-level intercession remains hidden and restricted to a few well-trained and highly anointed intercessors. But Satan is moving his attack plans against the Jewish people from being covert and primarily hidden to now being overt attacks. These overt attacks revealed his true purposes, which are the destruction of Israel and the extermination of the Jewish people.

This is what now requires a parallel shift in the work of intercession and spiritual warfare. Previously, much of this hidden work took place away from public view. However, since the Hamas Massacre of Jews was a globally published event, we must now move to a more public expression. Further, I believe God is calling us now to publicly announce His intentions of defeating the curse of genocide spoken and acted against the Jewish people. That is why this book, exposing these dangers and giving the prayer strategies we are called to deploy, is going out into the public domain.

Because this audience is much broader than only those who have been through equipping for strategic-level intercession and spiritual warfare, I have the pastoral concern that unequipped people may put themselves at greater risk by seeking to engage these high-level entities. So, if you are being called to join in this urgent prayer battle to prevent this evil from growing, and I certainly hope you are, please keep the following in mind:

First, implementing the following prayer strategies should not be undertaken alone or in your own strength. Instead, you should apply Jesus' guidelines for empowered prayer.

These are as follows:

- Asking and Receiving in Faith— Mark 11:22-24, Matthew 17:20-21

- The Importance of Forgiveness— Mark 11:25

- Praying In the Name of Jesus— John 14:12-14, Acts 3:1-10

- Amen - If Two Agree— Matthew 18:19-20

- Persistence— Luke 11:8

- Authority in Christ for Binding and Loosing— Matthew 18:18, Mark 3:13, John 20:23

Second, when binding the powers of darkness and asking for God's intervention, do it with groups of born-again believers, among whom Jesus Christ has promised to be present.

Third, when you engage in this vital work of cooperation with the Holy Spirit in defeating Satan's plans and praying for God's Kingdom to come, do so only in the authority given to us by Jesus Christ.

For your own safety, please keep these principles in mind as you seek to engage in this work of intercession and spiritual warfare. We hope many of you are being called to this level of intercession. If so, then we do have some excellent equipping that may help you grow in these areas, as well as connecting you with a global community of other intercessors who are called to this work. You can check this out on PRMI's website at www.prmi.org. You may also want to go to www.discernwith.us for more information on strategic-level intercession. There are many other ministries and prayer movements that the Lord has raised up to join in this battle and they, too, offer excellent equipping and teaching on these topics.

With these caveats, but not without reservations concerning the dangers involved, we are putting this prayer call out far and wide in the hope that the Lord will use this book to call forth the intercessors to overcome the evil that has been unleased in the October 7th, Hamas Massacre of Jews.

Summary: Pointers for Praying

As we pray, we must recognize both physical and spiritual reality. Prayer influences both realities. While our primary focus is spiritual, the effect of those prayers will change physical reality. Moses, Aaron, and Hur dealt with spiritual forces acting in and through the Amalekites. They also prayed for Joshua, who was in the midst of the physical battle. So, prayer must cover the spiritual realities of what's happening and protect the "Joshuas" engaging in ideological, political, and military conflicts.

God's heart is for everyone who is involved in this conflict, Jew or Palestinian, Hamas terrorist or IDF soldier. God is concerned with their eternal salvation and their relationship with Him. The work and power of the cross can save those who respond to the pull of the Spirit and repent. Sometimes, that can be challenging as we are often tempted to take sides. We need to remember that God is bigger than this conflict.

Here are some suggestions for ways to respond in prayer and intercession during the events that are taking place. As always, believers should allow their prayers to be directed by the Holy Spirit.

- Pray for the Lord to search your heart and remove any ungodly attitudes that may be present.

- Pray that the Lord would fill you with His perfect love so you can see the people and situations through His eyes.

- Pray about where and how the Lord is calling you to pray. Ask him to place you in the right group of intercessors to help you discern, pray, and intercede.

- Ask for His Holy Spirit's empowerment to intercede.

- Intercessors frequently are called to pray for God's mercy for everyone involved in this conflict. Pray that the Lord will show mercy to everyone involved in this conflict.

9

Announcing: God is at War with Hamas and Others Cursing Israel

When a nation goes to war, it is declared publicly. When God declared war against Amalek, the following public statements were made:

> Adonai said to Moses, "**Write this for a memorial in the book**, and rehearse it in the hearing of Joshua, for I will utterly blot out the memory of the Amalekites from under heaven." (15) Then **Moses built an altar**, and called the name of it Adonai-Nissi. (16) Then he said, "By the hand upon the throne of Adonai, **Adonai will have war with Amalek from generation to generation**." (Exodus 17:14-16 TLV)

This was the equivalent of a public declaration of war in that period.

After the October 7th, 2023, invasion and massacre, Prime Minister Benjamin Netanyahu made this statement announcing that Israel was at war:

> "Citizens of Israel, we are at war. Not an operation, not a round [of fighting] at war! This morning, Hamas initiated a murderous surprise attack against the state of

Chapter 9 Announcing: God is at War with Hamas and Others Cursing Israel

Israel and its citizens," Netanyahu said in his filmed statement in Hebrew.

"Hamas made a grave mistake this morning and started a war against the State of Israel. IDF soldiers are fighting the enemy at all the infiltration sites," Gallant said in remarks provided by his office.
"The State of Israel will win this war," he added.[48]

Now, in the case of fighting this present manifestation of Amalek, the IDF is the point of the spear. But those nations such as the USA and UK that have materially and morally supported them are also a part of it. All this is in the human and political realm, but Prime Minister Netanyahu vividly brought in the spiritual aspect – naming this connection with Amalek as enemies of the Jewish people and thus enemies of God. Here is a report from a speech by the Prime Minister providing the in-depth meaning of the war.

"You must remember what Amalek has done to you, says our Holy Bible. We do remember, and we are fighting," Netanyahu said in an address on Saturday.
"Our brave troops and combatants who are now in Gaza or around Gaza and in all other regions in Israel are joining this chain of Jewish heroes, a chain that started 3,000 years ago from Joshua ben Nun until the heroes of 1948, the Six-Day War, the '73 October War and all other wars in this country," he said.
"Our hero troops have one supreme main goal: to completely defeat the murderous enemy and to guarantee our existence in this country. We've always

---

[48] https://www.timesofisrael.com/we-are-at-war-netanyahu-says-after-hamas-launches-devastating-surprise-attack/

said never again. Never again is now," Netanyahu said.[49]

We cannot just spiritualize this battle that is taking place. It involves the use of military force and the killing of those who have chosen the way of death to impose the devil's vision of exterminating the Jewish people and destroying Israel. Because of Hamas' detestable and cruel practice of using civilians as human shields, this has included the loss of many civilian lives.

Our role as intercessors is to make explicit what the Bible says and to announce as a prophetic declaration what a politician must be more circumspect on, namely that God, according to His Word, has declared war against Hamas and all others who are cursing the Jews with genocide.

The Prophetic Declaration: Adonai is at War with Hamas and with All Who Side with Them in Cursing Israel

We announce that the God revealed in the Holy Bible is at war in the spiritual and earthly realms against all who have taken the role of Amalek by cursing the Jewish people and attacking them.

We make this prophetic declaration that "Adonai is at War" based on God's promise to Abraham and his descendants that "He will bless those who bless you and curse those who curse you" (Genesis 12:3), and on the basis that He has declared War from

---

[49] https://www.westernjournal.com/netanyahu-drops-old-testament-message-hamas-reminds-god-store-wicked-amalek/

Chapter 9 Announcing: God is at War with Hamas and Others Cursing Israel

Generation to Generation against Amalek (Exodus 17). This applies to all who "do not fear God" and who embody Amalek by seeking the destruction of Israel and the extermination of the Jews.

This Declaration of War, prophetically spoken in the spiritual realm, releases God's judgment against those who launched the October 7th invasion of Israel and the massacre that followed; against all those others, including university presidents, deceived, woke college students, Marxist movements like BLM, the UN and the nations who are joining in speaking the curse of genocide of the Jews by supporting Hamas; and against those who are opposing Israel's just war with Hamas.

We announce to Hamas and all who join them that God is at war with you because you have chosen to make the extermination of the Jews your goal and your policy.

We announce that, according to your policy of extermination and shedding innocent blood, you have intentionally violated the first law given to all humanity after the flood in God's Covenant with Noah, "The one who sheds human blood, by a human will his blood be shed, for in God's image He made humanity." (Genesis 9:6 TLV).

Making the murder of Jews a policy, as Hamas and other Islamist groups have, is very different from reacting in self-defense and removing those who have chosen to exterminate you, your family, your nation, and indeed your whole race.

Further, we announce that because Hamas and others have rejected life and have chosen the way of death for Jews, God intends that they will be destroyed.

As intercessors, we are called to follow the example of Moses praying for Joshua in the field while he was fighting the Amalekites. We are called to pray for all those whom God is choosing as His means to destroy those who threaten genocide of the Jewish people and of those engrafted into them through Yeshua.

Implications of this Declaration of War

This declaration that "Adonai is at war with Amalek" has profound implications. It means that all of us, whether intercessors or "Joshua workers," are called onto a war footing. We must identify the natural and supernatural enemies that God is waging war against and then join Him in His battle.

Further, while we all must hope and pray for peace, we must recognize that true peace can only come when those threatening genocide either repent of their plans or are utterly defeated. To call for peace, as many are presently doing, when that objective of complete victory has not yet been achieved is to create the conditions for the next outbreak of evil - usually more deadly than the last one. Many people, some well-intended and others not, serve as false prophets saying, "peace when there is no peace." Ezekiel condemns them because the result will be future disaster:

> "Precisely because they have led My people astray saying, 'Shalom' when there is no shalom, they build a weak wall, behold, they plaster it over with whitewash. Say to those who plaster it over with whitewash, that it will fall. There will be a downpouring rain, and on you great hailstones will fall, and a storm wind will break out. Behold, when the wall has fallen, will it not be said about you, 'Where is the whitewash that you plastered it with?'" (Ezekiel 13:10-12 TLV)

To call for peace prematurely, or to force Israel to settle for anything less than either the unconditional surrender of Hamas or their destruction, will only contribute to an even greater future disaster for Israel and the Jewish people.

As intercessors we must recognize that now is the time for war! Our role is to pray that those present-day manifestations of Amalek, against whom God has declared war, will be defeated. For some this means fighting on bloody battlefields. For us, as intercessors cooperating with the guidance of the Holy Spirit, it means joining with Jesus in engaging the demonic powers. At the very same time, we must persist in praying that these Jihadists will

Chapter 9 Announcing: God is at War with Hamas and Others Cursing Israel

be encountered by Jesus Christ, and that their hatred will be turned to love so that the broken family of Abraham may be healed.

God's Judgment Includes the Destruction of Those Who Threaten Genocide to His People.

Many may be tempted to minimize the severity of God's judgment against those like the Hamas Jihadis who have chosen the destruction of Israel and the extermination of the Jewish people as their raison d'être, especially for the sake of the many innocent people who will suffer or be killed in the process. However, we must also recognize that in some cases of intractable evil, both God's justice and the completion of His redemptive plans may require the destruction of those demonic strongholds and the people who embody them.

This was the case in the Old Testament demonic stronghold that had formed around the people of Amalek, who did not fear God – they had to be destroyed (Exodus 17:8-16). The same was true for the core of the Nazi totalitarian demonic stronghold – it had to be destroyed by the combined military might of the United Kingdom, the Soviet Union, and the United States. I believe that this is also the case with the core of the demonic stronghold of Hamas, who do not fear God and have dedicated themselves to the destruction of Israel and of the Jewish people. Like the Amalekites, they must be destroyed. As intercessors, we are called to pray for their salvation but, if they refuse God's grace, we must pray for their destruction.

We Announce That Through Jesus Christ, God the Father Almighty Extends His Grace and Forgiveness to All — Which, if Received, Will Result in Life, but if Rejected, Will Lead to Everlasting Death.

This announcement of God's judgment which many will find severe is intended bring both individuals and indeed whole nations, to repentance and salvation, Jesus Christ. God himself announces this purpose of His judgments through His prophet Jeremiah:

> At one moment I may speak about a nation or about a kingdom, to uproot, to pull down or to destroy it. But if that nation turns from their evil, because of what I have spoken against it, I will relent concerning the calamity that I planned to do to it. (Jer 18:7-8 TLV)

This repentance may take place in many ways, as for instance turning away from the agenda of destroying Israel to cooperating with Israel, which shifts the balance away from the curse to God's blessings. This will be blessing in the human realm resulting in prosperity and peace.

The ultimate blessing which we are called to pray for is that this turning from curse to blessing will result in coming to salvation. Which is only through Jesus Christ.

> "...There is salvation in no one else, for there is no other name under heaven given to mankind by which we must be saved!" Act 4:12 TLV

The desire for mercy and love for all people is the underlying motivation of God the Father's heart, revealed in Jesus Christ. This makes it imperative that we should join in praying for their salvation.

God's judgment, manifested in His Declaration of War against the present embodiments of Amalek, is not only for destruction, but is also intended to bring people to repentance and to faith in Jesus Christ. It also has the role of destroying the structures of evil that have enslaved many innocent people and coerced them into their evil plans. This is what has happened in Gaza under the hate-filled reign of Hamas. They have enslaved nearly the entire population of Gaza through constant indoctrination and

Chapter 9 Announcing: God is at War with Hamas and Others Cursing Israel

totalitarian control. They have tortured and murdered anyone who has dared to oppose them.[50] Destroying this insidious evil political and ideological system will be the means of setting people free from this bondage.

However, what if Hamas leaders, the foot soldiers, and all those who join them, do not repent and renounce their stated policy of genocide of the Jewish people? In that case, God has declared that He will annihilate them. So far, there is little indication of any repentance or turning away from these goals. Instead, we found the following:

> "A senior member of Hamas [Ghazi Hamad] has hailed the systematic slaughter of civilians in Israel on October 7, vowing in an interview that if given the chance, the Palestinian terror group will repeat similar assaults many times in the future until Israel is exterminated."[51]

Our role as intercessors will be praying for the Joshua workers through whom God will wipe out the memory of Amalek. We must also pray against all those forces that are seeking to intervene because they want to prevent the Israeli military from accomplishing this purpose of destroying Hamas and its other adversaries who are threatening genocide.

When intercessors are called into this war that God has declared against Amalek, there is a significant assignment that I believe we are called to undertake. This is first exposing and then, in

---

[50] See the following book for a powerful confirmation of the true nature of Hamas as a demonic stronghold with totalitarian control over its members and the subjugated people of Gaza. *Son of Hamas: A Gripping Account of Terror, Betrayal, Political Intrigue, and Unthinkable Choices* – Unabridged, March 2, 2010 - by Mosab Hassan Yousef (Author), Ron Brackin (Contributor)

[51] https://www.timesofisrael.com/hamas-official-says-group-aims-to-repeat-oct-7-onslaught-many-times-to-destroy-israel/

cooperation with Jesus Christ, breaking the curses of genocide spoken against the Jewish People.

Summary: Pointers for Praying

There are consequences for our actions. This reality is true both physically and spiritually. We find ourselves under God's judgment when we do not follow God's ways. Those who seek the destruction of the Jews and Israel, just like the Amalekites, come under God's judgment. When they choose death as the means of achieving their goal, then death is a consequence, and they face destruction.

This is not just focused on Hamas. We all fall short of God's standards and are under His judgment. That includes Israel, and it includes us personally as well as nationally. As Paul reminds us, "For all have sinned and fall short of the glory of God." (Romans 3:23)

The gospel message declares that mercy and forgiveness are possible in Christ, and so there is hope. There is an opportunity for redemption for anyone. It is this gospel reality that provides us the foundation for our prayer.

Here are some suggestions for ways to respond in prayer and intercession during the events that are taking place. As always, believers should allow their prayers to be directed by the Holy Spirit.

- We pray for the exposure of those at the heart of the stronghold of Hamas. These leaders need either to repent or be removed. So, pray that they will encounter God's

Chapter 9 Announcing: God is at War with Hamas and Others Cursing Israel

mercy, realize that they are under God's judgment, and turn instead to Jesus, who offers forgiveness.

- We pray for true peace, which will happen when the evil system of the Hamas organization is removed. This organization has enslaved Palestinians and caused so much death and misery to Jews and Palestinians alike. Pray that the Lord would remove the organization and its influence within Gaza.

- We pray for those who, out of naivete or woke deception, have blindly been calling for Israel's destruction. Pray that they encounter the truth, receive it, and turn from the lies.

- We pray that demonic forces clouding, confusing, and blocking people from seeing the truth will be removed. Pray that the scales over people's eyes will be removed so that they can know the truth.

10

Breaking the Curses of Genocide

We have affirmed that God has declared war against the present-day expressions of Amalek – those who do not fear God and seek to destroy Israel and exterminate the Jewish people. As part of this declaration of war, the Lord calls us as intercessors to take part with Him in breaking the curse of genocide. This is the key, vital assignment and is the reason for my being called to write this short book. Exposing and breaking this curse is essential not only in achieving victory in the war, but also in preparing the way for the great outpouring of the Holy Spirit. God is sending this outpouring to enable the Gospel of the Kingdom to go to all nations, including "all Israel" being saved through Yeshua the Messiah (Romans 11:25-26).

Observations About the Nature and Function of Curses

First, we must recognize that these curses were embodied not just in the spoken words but also in the horrible actions that took place on October 7th, the Hamas Massacre of the Jews. These words and actions and the pictures of their atrocities sent out over the internet are being utilized by Satan as death curses released against Israel and the Jewish people. The Oct 7th Hamas Massacre of the Jews was – and still is being – amplified by the

Chapter 10 Breaking the Curses of Genocide

words of those protesting against Israel and calling for the murder of Jews. Let's review the different aspects of how these words and actions function as curses.

The Barbaric Actions Which Were Graphically Broadcasted Serve as Curses Because They Fulfill the Original Curses Against Jews Spoken by Mohammed.

Let's review one aspect of the Jihadist actions that many find inexplicable, which I wrote earlier in the book.

On October 7, 2023, Hamas, the terrorist organization that controls Gaza, launched a massive, coordinated, surprise attack that came over land, sea, and air—with over 5000 rockets shot into Israel. The worst part was that the Islamic jihadists broke through the security barriers, entering many Israeli villages and kibbutzim and murdering over 1300 men, women, and children.

Jihadists, joined by a larger number of civilians from Gaza, gunned down entire groups of innocent people, beheaded children and babies, gang-raped women and children, and burned alive whole families in their homes. Grisly evidence revealed children and families were tortured to death. Like marauding Orcs, they dragged several hundred men, women, and children back to Gaza. What is more, the murderers gleefully posted the graphic, gory atrocities on the internet, replete with the background screams of their victims and the Islamists shouting, "Allahu Akbar," "Allah is Greater!" They also used their victims' cell phones to post their diabolical and barbaric brutality to the victims' Facebook pages so that families could watch the brutality.

How do we explain this gruesome behavior? It is terrible enough that they committed such barbaric acts against fellow human beings, but then why proudly broadcast their bloody work over the internet for all the world to see? Hamas has often been compared to the Nazis, but there are some notable differences that may lead to a deeper understanding of what the Devil is doing through them.

Author Douglas Murray says the comparisons between the Nazis and Hamas are insufficient after seeing the raw footage from October 7th. Mr. Murray joined Sky News Australia host Piers Morgan to discuss what he had seen while traveling through several sites of the October 7 terror attack by Hamas.

> "Even the Nazis were ashamed at what they did; SS battalions who spent their days shooting Jews in the back of the head and pushing them into trenches had to get very, very drunk in the evening to forget what they had done," he said. "Nazi high command famously had to get around the problem of soldier morale because the soldiers knew this wasn't exactly what their lives were meant to look like either.
>
> "I'll tell you one very big difference. If you look at the raw footage ... that is at least as barbaric as the Nazis did but here's the difference – they did it with glee; they were deeply proud."[52]

In the case of the Nazis, the curse of genocide against the Jews was not spoken of and amplified by showing the actual horror of carrying out the curse. Instead, this curse had been spoken in Hitler's frenzied speeches in the Nuremberg Rallies calling for a Jew-free Europe. The actions activating the curse took place in events such as the boycott against Jewish goods of 1933 and the night of Broken Glass in 1938, but the actual goal of mass murder of millions of innocent people created in the image of God was almost always cloaked. The actual plans were masked behind

---

[52] 'They did it with glee': Douglas Murray says Nazi comparisons insufficient for Hamas November 09, 2023 - 10:01AM
https://www.skynews.com.au/opinion/piers-morgan/they-did-it-with-glee-douglas-murray-says-nazi-comparisons-insufficient-for-hamas/video/32e04228e20bae8d124f1d40cb474777

Chapter 10 Breaking the Curses of Genocide

euphemisms like the "Jewish Problem"" or the "Final Solution of the Jewish Question." The fact that Hamas has not hidden their plans but celebrated them and publicly stated them both in their charter and public pronouncements demonstrates that there is a different dynamic at work than in the Nazis.

I believe the difference is found in the fact that Germany's cultural roots are in Christianity, both Roman Catholic and Protestant. In that context, the call for the murder of innocent people, which is entirely contrary to biblical faith, must be hidden. But Hamas grows out of Islam, where the killing of Jews and Christians is not only sanctioned but commanded by their prophet. We have already clearly demonstrated that there are many texts in the Koran and the Hadith that Satan has used to deceive faithful Muslims into his plans for the genocide of Jews and Christians.

What these Jihadists were doing and celebrating was the fulfillment of the curses that had already been spoken against the Jewish people by their prophet. Satan is now taking the combination of the words of the Koran and the Hadith, and the images and videos of what Hamas calls the "true Muslim" carrying out those words and is employing them as a curse to build faith in Islam and release even more evil. By their acts of violence and hatred, they prove they are following the example of Mohammed in obedience to the Koran. I have already cited these texts, but we must quote them again because the atrocities that were committed do indeed embody and fulfill the commands. To quote just two examples:

- "Terrorize and behead those who believe in scriptures other than the Qur'an." (Koran 8:12)

- "Muslims must muster all weapons to terrorize the infidels." (Koran 8:60)[53]

---

[53] I got this summary from the following site
http://www.nairaland.com/1283381/these-verses-really-quran

Satan then uses these curses, and the faith they generate, to draw into the demonic strongholds other Muslims who have the seeds of deception already sown in their hearts. The result is that both the individuals and the organization are granted demonic and earthly power to carry out Satan's purposes. In this case, it is the extermination of Jews just because they are Jews.

These curses calling for killing Jews must be broken; otherwise, they will continue to grow and, like a cancer metastasizing into every part of the body, will be used by Satan to implement his terrible purposes. This has already happened in Gaza, but Satan plans to release this curse of genocide against the Jews globally. To accomplish this, he must ignite Jew-hatred worldwide in preparation for fulfilling the curse of genocide.

Genocide Starts with Hatred

Carrying out the plans for genocide does not begin with the acts of mayhem, murder, rape, and torture that the Hamas jihadists committed against Jewish men, women, and children. It begins with hatred of Jews in their hearts. Stirring up hatred is Satan's first step in his campaign of murder. The first letter of John starkly tells us why hatred is the initial step.

> Do not be surprised, brothers and sisters, if the world hates you. We know that we have passed from death to life because we love our brothers and sisters. The one who does not love remains in death. Everyone who hates his brother is a murderer—and you know that no murderer has eternal life abiding in him. We have come to know love by this—Yeshua laid down His life for us, and we also ought to lay down our lives for our brothers and sisters. (1 John 3:13-16 TLV)

> The one who says he is in the light and hates his brother is still in the darkness. The one who loves his

> brother abides in the light, and in him there is no cause for stumbling. But whoever hates his brother is in the darkness and walks in the darkness. He doesn't know where he is going, because the darkness has made his eyes blind. (1 John 2:9-11 TLV)

Hatred of others, whether it is justified or not, opens us up to being demonized and to being blinded and deceived. In this way, the stirring up of hatred is always the precursor and necessary preparation for people to be deceived into courses of actions that may lead to murder. So, part of the curse of genocide against the Jews is first to stir up hatred of them. What is happening now is an example of this.

We are also already seeing how the October 7th Massacre has ignited expressions of Jew-hatred worldwide. There are calls for Holocaust 2.0 and for completion of the work that Hitler started. Already, these events have inflamed hatred of Jews, and they carry the potential to escalate the outbreaks of evil worldwide, far beyond the boundaries of Israel and Gaza.

The massive increase of antisemitism and expressions of Jew-hatred in the United States of America since the October 7th Massacre demonstrates how Satan uses this type of event to stir up a contagion of evil. Here is a report from the Algemeiner newsletter:

> "Antisemitic incidents in the US rose by an eye-watering 360 percent in the period since the Oct. 7 Hamas pogrom in southern Israel reignited the conflict in the Middle East, according to new data released on Wednesday by the Anti-Defamation League (ADL)."
>
> "The American Jewish community is facing a threat level that's now unprecedented in modern history," Greenblatt warned. "It's shocking that we've recorded more antisemitic acts in three months than we usually

would in an entire year."

"The breakdown of incidents includes 60 episodes of physical assault and 553 acts of vandalism. More than 1,000 pro-Hamas rallies featured antisemitic rhetoric."

"In this difficult moment, antisemitism is spreading and mutating in alarming ways," Greenblatt said. "This onslaught of hate includes a dramatic increase in fake bomb threats that disrupt services at synagogues and put communities on edge across the country."[54] The fact that these acts of Jew-hatred are being seen in many locations is a sign that this curse of genocide is indeed spreading, and that Satan is using hatred to prepare people to take part in his deadly plans.

The first step to overcoming this plague of antisemitism is to recognize its ideological roots in the antichrist ideologies of Islam and Marxism. This must be denounced, as many are thankfully doing. This is a good starting place, but the roots of Jew-hatred are spiritual and come from Satan, who hates God and the people of God. This hatred finds a ready welcome in the unredeemed, sinful human heart. Educational programs and legal actions can only go so far, because a spiritual problem requires a spiritual solution. Truly, the only way to overcome Jew-hatred is through a movement of the Holy Spirit bringing people to Yeshua the Messiah, for only He can transform the human heart. Only in Jesus can there be the forgiveness and healing needed to overcome the deep wounds of the past and present, which makes way for hatred to be replaced with love.

This work of breaking curses of genocide is intended only to remove the obstacles for the Gospel to go forth. Curse-breaking is not the fundamental solution to Jew-hatred in the human

---

[54] Antisemitic Incidents Rocketing in US Since Hamas Pogrom, New ADL Data Shows JANUARY 10, 2024 8:00 AM2 by Ben Cohen
https://www.algemeiner.com/2024/01/10/antisemitic-incidents-rocketing-us-since-hamas-pogrom-new-adl-data-shows/

heart. Only Jesus Christ is the solution! Yet even when people have been born-again, the tragic history of antisemitism and bigotry in the Christian church demonstrates that true heart transformation can only be wrought by Jesus Christ, Yeshua Ha Mashiach, through the empowering working of the Holy Spirit, and through being rooted in the Holy Bible as the word of God. Only then are we enabled, by God's own Spirit dwelling within us, to live into the reality of the reconciliation between Jew and Gentile that has been bought by Jesus' blood on the cross. (Ephesians 2:13-16)

YESHUA the CURSE REVERSER - God Uses Blessing to Cancel Curses[55]

From the beginning, starting with the call of Abraham in Genesis 12, God conceived the nation of his descendants and its spiritual counterpart, the Church of Jesus Christ, as an instrument to both give and receive blessings that reach to all peoples on the earth.

> "I will make you into a great nation, and I will bless you; I will make your name great and you will be a blessing. I will bless those who bless you, and whoever curses you I will curse; and all peoples on earth will be blessed through you." (Genesis 12:2,3)

God not only bestows blessings, but he also reverses curses. The best example is that Jesus the Messiah was wounded, not by or because of our sins, but *for* our sins.

> "But he was pierced for our transgressions, he was

---

[55] This section is by Steve Aceto.

crushed for our iniquities; the punishment that brought us peace was on him, and by his wounds we are healed" (Isaiah 53:5).

In other words, the Messiah took the curse that rightly was on us and reversed it by taking it on himself "for" our sins.

Another example is when Israel was on their journey to the land promised to Abraham, the tribes hired Balaam, a prophet and seer, to curse them from a high vantage point. Try as he might, Balaam was not only physically unable to pronounce curses, but he actually pronounced blessings to the great consternation of his employers.

> Then he uttered his oracle and said, "From Aram, Balak brought me, Moab's king from the mountains of the east: 'Come! Curse Jacob for me! 'Come! Denounce Israel!' How can I curse one whom God has not cursed? How can I denounce one whom Adonai has not denounced? (Numbers 23:7-8 TLV)

Interestingly, even the animals know there is a blessing on Israel. On one occasion a donkey would go no further after seeing a vision of God's avenging angel and spoke aloud to his master of the blessing on Israel. The curse that God reversed in favor of Israel does not neglect to mention Israel's enemies. "May those who bless you be blessed and those who curse you be cursed," and "Amalek was first among the nations, but their end will be utter destruction" (Numbers 24:9, 20).

This brings us not just to generational curses but also to generational blessings, specifically in relation to the nation now known as Iran. Consider Iran, a modern nation that is spiritually identified with Old Testament Persia. Cyrus, the Persian ruler, blessed the Jews by defeating the Babylonian kingdom which had visited destruction upon Jerusalem in 586 BC.

Isaiah had prophesied that God would give the Jews favor in the eyes of Cyrus, going so far as to name him a "shepherd" of

Chapter 10 Breaking the Curses of Genocide

God's people. In the books of Ezra, Jeremiah, and Daniel, this blessing is fulfilled. Cyrus was compelled to restore to the Jews the treasures of the temple, which had been plundered by the Babylonians. He also released the Jews to rebuild the temple, that they might make intercession before their God for Cyrus and his family.

Conflict in the spiritual realm of principalities then spilled over to the physical realm of nations. Daniel reported that an angel who was seeking to reach him in Babylon (in modern day Iraq) was detained by the Prince of Persia, who is identified as another spiritual being. Perhaps this is an archetype of Satan standing against God's intended blessing on a nation. Maybe it is time to ask our Heavenly Father to release Persia so that the nation may bless the Jews once again. Now seems appropriate that the intercessors pray into God's purposes for Persia – Iran – that it would be released as a nation and that a new "Cyrus" would once again bless the Jews. We should also pray that the Jews would, in return bless Persia by interceding for Iran, as they once did for Cyrus and his family.

Jesus' Guidelines for Breaking Curses

When it comes to breaking the curses of genocide, there are biblical guidelines that must be carefully followed lest we experience unintended negative consequences. This is especially true when breaking a curse of this nature - deep hatreds with ancient roots in the original wounding between Sarah and Hagar and their two sons, Isaac and Ishmael. Let us make sure that we are well-grounded before proceeding. First, be aware of and diligently seek to apply the five guidelines for all effective prayer, which must be:

1. In relationship with Jesus Christ (John 15:4-5, 7-8, I John 5:14-15)
2. In the name of Jesus (John 14:12-14, Acts 3:1-10)
3. In agreement with one another (Matthew 18:19-20)

4. Asking and receiving in faith (Mark 11:22-24, Matthew 17:20-21)
5. Led by the Holy Spirit. (Romans 8:26-27)

We must add to these some specific instructions for breaking curses.

First, we must recognize that the spiritual origin of curses is either God or Satan, but that they are often mediated through people. Here, we shall address the topic of curses that come from Satan, which the Holy Spirit is calling us to break because they are being activated against the Lord, His plans, or His people. When we are breaking curses from the devil regarding the human beings through whom they are given, Jesus also expects us to adhere to the following directions:

- "But I say to you who are listening: Love your enemies, do good to those who hate you, bless those who curse you, pray for those who mistreat you." (Luke 6:27-28)

- Bless those who persecute you, bless and do not curse. (Romans 12:14)

- Do not avenge yourselves, dear friends, but give place to God's wrath, for it is written, "Vengeance is mine, I will repay," says the Lord. (Romans 12:19)

The primary rule here is not to curse back but instead to bless those who are doing the cursing. This sounds like an impossible task! When we deal with an event like the October 7th Hamas Massacre of the Jews, which embodied and disseminated Jew-hatred and the curse of the genocide of the Jews worldwide, it is a terrible struggle to bring ourselves to bless the perpetrators. I know that when I saw the images of what the Jihadists did to those innocent people, it was all I could do not to curse them back. But to do so is to play right into Satan's hands and to open the door for him to work through us. The key to not doing this is

Chapter 10 Breaking the Curses of Genocide

as follows:

- First, forgive these people.
- Second, be guided by the Holy Spirit to know how He wants us to bless them and be committed to being the means of blessing.
- Third, release all vengeance back to the Lord.
- Fourth, be committed to being the means the Lord may use to exact His vengeance.

To act on these principles in the midst of the struggle is a lot easier said than done. To illustrate them, I offer the example of what took place during the October 12-16, 2023, Mountain Top Equipping Camp[56]. This gathering at the Community of the Cross in North Carolina took place right after the October 7th Massacre. We had about 40 people involved in a time of strategic-level intercession. We were all reeling from the Massacre. We were led to pray intensely for the leaders of Hamas and to break the curse of genocide against the Jews that had catalyzed and ignited Jew-hatred in multiple locations worldwide. We put up on the screen pictures of the Hamas leaders who were celebrating the carnage inflicted on Israel and calling for jihad against Israel and the Jews.

Adhering to Yeshua's guidelines for praying for these Hamas leaders with their bloody hands was difficult for all of us who love Israel and the Jewish people. It was most difficult for the Jewish members of our group, who carried within their lineage the searing memories of the Holocaust. We had an extended period of confessing our sins and the sins of Israel and America.

Then Grant Berry, who is Jewish, led us into a time of praying for the Hamas leaders. With tears, he asked the Lord to forgive them and then, in mercy, to bring them to faith in Yeshua, the

---

[56] Our Mountain Top Equipping Camps draw their title from the example of Moses on the mountain, interceding for Joshua and the Israelite army as they battled the Amalekites.

Messiah. This was an enormous struggle for Grant. We all joined in this with him. Expressing this type of forgiveness and love and not cursing but blessing is not humanly possible. We were only enabled to do this by the presence of the Holy Spirit, who prayed through us and empowered us to do what Jesus would do.

Later in this prayer event, the Lord blessed the entire group, especially Grant, with joy and laughter, which was cleansing and healing. We then were led to break, in the name of Jesus, the curses of genocide that had been unleashed upon the Jewish people. Further, we were anointed to pray that the Israeli military, who were in the role of "Joshua," would be enabled to remove the leaders of Hamas and destroy the terrorist group's ability to carry out their campaign of extermination. We have also been praying for the release of the hostages.

In March of 2024, we are still praying for these leaders to come to repentance or, at God's direction, for them to be removed. We have seen many answers to our prayers, with some hostages being released and terrorist leaders being killed. But war still rages, both in the spiritual as well as human realm. The conflict seems to be spreading, with Iran's other proxies joining in.

From my own experience in breaking curses, I have added another principle:

A curse must be broken in the same medium in which the curse was released.

This is based not so much on examples from the Bible but on understanding the overall dynamic of divine/human cooperation. Essentially, God works in the world through His Word, which may be spoken or written. When His Word is received in faith and then acted on in obedience, it is empowered by the Holy Spirit to accomplish its intent. We have already noted how this dynamic is at work, with Satan using curses to achieve his purpose. This is why the Hamas terrorists posted gory images of their atrocities, fulfilling the commands of

Chapter 10 Breaking the Curses of Genocide

Allah in the Koran. When these are received in faith and acted upon, they are demonically empowered and draw others into participation.

The critical thing to note is that both God's words and Satan's words are expressed through human beings via different media. Initially, words were verbally spoken, visually acted out, displayed in art and on monuments, or written. We now add the role of all the communications posted on the internet, whether as images, videos or in writing. Such "speaking" of God's words or Satan's curses, through whatever medium, has an impact in both the human realm and the spiritual realm.

For instance, prayers of God's people given in faith, in the name of Jesus Christ, and empowered by the Holy Spirit may inspire the actions of others who are receiving guidance from the Holy Spirit or may mobilize the angelic hosts under Christ's command. When we speak these words verbally, publicly or in a private prayer gathering, we provide the Holy Spirit with what He needs to do God's work. This happened when an angel was sent to bring Peter out of prison in answer to the earnest, faithful prayers of the church (Acts 5). A similar dynamic is at work for Satan to accomplish his evil on earth. His words, which are most often lies, must be spoken through various media, received in faith, acted upon, and empowered by the demonic to function as curses.

Let's apply this to the breaking of curses. It leads us to counter Satan's curses in the same medium that they are given. This is what led us to the publication of this book and to being called to make these prophetic declarations and break the curses online. When empowered by the Holy Spirit, our words and actions impact both the human and spiritual realms.

The principle is that we must break the curse in the same medium in which the curse was released and recognize that we are speaking through these different media both to the human and to the spiritual realms. So, for example, if a curse is given in a video over the Internet, then the Lord may call us to break it in a video over the Internet.

As we seek by prayer to "return evil with good" and to break the curses, those in bondage to the stronghold of Islam may speak against us. I suggest the following:

- When they curse us with death, we must denounce these words as being from the devil and not from God and declare firmly what Jesus Christ says of himself: "I am the way, and the truth, and the life. No one comes to the Father except through me". (John 14:6)

- When they announce that Islam will rule the world, we must denounce that as a lie from Satan and instead proclaim the good news of the Gospel and declare that Jesus/Yeshua is the Lord of all the earth.

We announce the Father's inevitable victory in Jesus:

"As a result, God exalted him and gave him the name that is above every name, so that at the name of Jesus every knee will bow—in heaven and on earth and under the earth—and every tongue confess that Jesus Christ is Lord to the glory of God the Father." (Philippians 2:9-11)

- When they justify their atrocities as being the will of Allah and speak to us words from the Koran or the Hadith, we reject it all as lies from Satan. We break their power by declaring that humanity's truth, salvation, and destiny are found only in Jesus Christ.

- When Muhammad is announced as the final prophet and the fulfillment of the promise of Abraham, we announce the words of Jesus the Messiah, for "salvation is from the Jews" (John 4:22), and we boldly proclaim of Jesus Christ: "in Him all the promises of God are 'Yes.'" (2 Corinthians

1:20 TLV) and "...there is salvation in no one else, for there is no other name under heaven given among people by which we must be saved." (Acts 4:12)

- When Muslims announce the coming of the Islamic Jesus, who will break the cross, and the Mahdi, who will establish the Islamic Caliphate and worldwide Islamic hegemony, we must declare that these are the plans of Satan and not God, and that Yeshua/Jesus will indeed come again. We proclaim that Jesus Christ will come again in glory, that He has poured out His Holy Spirit, and through His born-again people is building the Kingdom of life and grace that brings justice and peace.

Breaking the Curse of Genocide Against the Jews Requires the Following Steps

The steps in breaking these curses are outlined in the following principles, which are based on what Jesus teaches us about curses and how to break them.

A principle of breaking curses is that they must be broken the same way they were communicated and broken by those in authority, whether political, cultural, or spiritual.

First: Exposing the Fact that Extermination of the Jews is the Agenda of Specific People, Groups, Movements and Governments, AND Publicly Denouncing Them as Evil.

Throughout history, Satan has hidden his true agenda, which is to replace God by murdering the Jewish people in order to annul the Covenants. Satan has also masterfully cloaked his plans for genocide because if they were exposed in all their barbaric evil, those with any conscience at all would recoil in horror.

Many are exposing and denouncing these agendas of the Jihadists and of those who are supporting them. For instance, the following statement was made by the deputy White House press secretary, Andrew Bates:

> "It's unbelievable that this needs to be said: calls for genocide are monstrous and antithetical to everything we represent as a country,"
> "Any statements that advocate for the systematic murder of Jews are dangerous and revolting — and we should all stand firmly against them, on the side of human dignity and the most basic values that unite us as Americans."[57]

The great constitutional lawyer Alan Dershowitz has written a book entitled War *Against the Jews: How to End Hamas Barbarism.* This was published on December 12, 2023, and is a public exposé and denunciation of the plans for the destruction of Israel and the genocide of the Jews by Hamas and those who support them.

Many commentators (some Jewish like Ben Shapiro, Andrew Klavan, and Dennis Prager) have exposed the evil intent of genocide over the internet and condemned it, as has the brilliant British author Douglas Murray, who went to Israel right after the massacre. His commentary has exposed the true purpose of the genocide of the Jewish people. Thankfully, there are many others from different political perspectives.

From the spiritual perspective, there have been words and commentary from Jewish leaders in Tikkun, especially Asher Intrater.

The Pope has made a statement in a letter to the Jews of Israel, publicly condemning hatred of Jews and Judaism and naming antisemitism as a sin.

VATICAN CITY (CNS) -- In a letter addressed to "my

---

[57] https://www.washingtonpost.com/politics/2023/12/06/white-house-university-presidents-antisemitism-genocide/

Chapter 10 Breaking the Curses of Genocide

Jewish brothers and sisters in Israel," Pope Francis expressed his heartbreak at the violence unleashed by the Hamas attack on Israel in October, and he repeated the Catholic Church's condemnation of all forms of antisemitism and anti-Judaism.

"The path that the Church has walked with you, the ancient people of the covenant, rejects every form of anti-Judaism and anti-Semitism, unequivocally condemning manifestations of hatred toward Jews and Judaism as a sin against God," said the letter dated Feb. 2 and released by the Vatican the next day.

"Together with you," he said, "we Catholics are very concerned about the terrible increase in attacks against Jews around the world. We had hoped that 'never again' would be a refrain heard by the new generations. Yet, now we see that the path ahead requires ever closer collaboration to eradicate these phenomena."[58]

This book that you hold in your hands is both an exposé of these plans for genocide and a denunciation of them.

This is when the Church of Jesus Christ must not and cannot remain silent. We must speak out the truth and expose and denounce as from the devil these curses of genocide which are being acted and spoken against the Jewish people. To be silent at this time because we are afraid of offending people, or because we are focused on our ministries, will contribute to conditions comparable to those of the 1930s when the church in Germany was primarily silent and did not break the curse of genocide. At the same time, there was still time to prevent the

---

[58] *Pope, in letter to Jews in Israel, condemns antisemitism as a sin,* https://www.usccb.org/news/2024/pope-letter-jews-israel-condemns-antisemitism-sin

Holocaust.

With the October 7th Hamas Massacre of the Jews, these plans of genocide were displayed for all the world to see and the true impact of the slogans, "From the river to the sea, Palestine will be free," has been exposed. If we, as Christians and Messianic Jews, remain silent as did the church in Germany, we will be contributing to and responsible for the evil that will undoubtedly follow. It will be said of us, as it was said of the church in Germany in the 1930s, "Silence in the face of evil is itself evil: God will not hold us guiltless. Not to speak is to speak. Not to act is to act."

These words, attributed to Dietrich Bonhoeffer, are a stark reminder of the consequences of the church's silence in the face of evil. The church at that time did have somewhat of an excuse. They did not know at the time what would be the full horrible implications of Jew-hatred going viral and unchecked, namely the Holocaust. But with the benefit of decades of historical hindsight, we do know that these demonic forces of evil that were exposed and unleashed in the October 7th Hamas Massacre of the Jews will lead to genocide if not exposed and defeated. We have no excuse! So, our silence would be even more damnable than that of the German Church.

So, we must speak out, naming the evil and the consequences. Doing so is part of the work of overcoming this curse of genocide against God's chosen people.

In Prayer Under the Anointing of the Holy Spirit and, in the Name of Jesus Christ, Formally Break the Curses Calling for Genocide of the Jews.

Here are some specific ways we have been led to pray by the Holy Spirit. We must speak these words in prayer among ourselves but also speak them over video and broadcast them into cyberspace, just as the Islamic Jihadists broadcast their terrible images over the internet. We speak these over the internet just as the images of protesters were posted. These are

Chapter 10 Breaking the Curses of Genocide

spoken not just to the human actors but to the evil spirits behind the people and movements.

Remember Jesus' words to do this in company – in groups of at least two or three – and do not curse back.

- In the authority of the mighty name of Jesus Christ, we break the power of these embodiments of the curse of the genocide of Jews in these images from the October 7th Massacre.

- In the name of Jesus Christ, we break the curses of genocide in calls for exterminating the Jewish people.

- In the name of Jesus Christ, we confuse and negate the schemes of Satan to use these words and images for his evil purposes, namely, to destroy the Jewish people.

- By the authority of the name of Jesus Christ, we overcome the curse of the slogan "From the River to the Sea Palestine will be free" and restore the promise given to Abraham by God Almighty, giving to him and his descendants the land,

We Announce that Adonai's Promises to Abraham will be Fulfilled.

- First, we affirm that God really did make a covenant with Abraham, really did promise the land to him, and declared that He would bless those who blessed him and his descendants and curse those who cursed him.

    We affirm these are promises that God has made out of His own Sovereign will and purpose.

    Then Adonai appeared to Abram and said, "I will give this land to your seed." So there he built an altar to

Adonai, who had appeared to him. Genesis 12:7 TLV

"On that day Adonai cut a covenant with Abram, saying, "I give this land to your seed, from the river of Egypt to the great river, the Euphrates River: the Kenite, the Kenizzites, the Kadmonites, the Hittites, the Perizzites, the Raphaites, the Amorites, the Canaanites, the Girgashites, and the Jebusites." (Genesis 15:18-21 TLV)

"My heart's desire is to make you into a great nation, to bless you, to make your name great so that you may be a blessing. My desire is to bless those who bless you, but whoever curses you I will curse, and in you all the families of the earth will be blessed." (Genesis 12:2-3 TLV)

"I will richly bless you and bountifully multiply your seed like the stars of heaven, and like the sand that is on the seashore, and your seed will possess the gate of his enemies. (18) In your seed all the nations of the earth will be blessed—because you obeyed My voice." (Genesis 22:17-18 TLV)

Here are suggested prayers for announcing this promise of Abraham:

- By the power of the One who has all authority in heaven and on earth, Jesus Christ, who gave us the command to "Make disciples of all nations," we break the strongholds of Satan's deception that would block the fulfillment of this command in nations that are under the bondage of Islam.

- We pray, Lord, that you would bring Hamas leaders to a saving knowledge of Jesus Christ. Lord Jesus, have mercy on their souls and the souls of all those over whom they have authority. Speak to them through visions or the means of your choosing, as you spoke to Saul, the Jewish persecutor of the Church, on the road to Damascus.

- Lord, for the sake of your chosen people, the Jews, and the Church of Jesus Christ, silence all those who are speaking curses against your people, the Jews and Israel, until the day his words become words of witness for Jesus! If they refuse your Grace, remove them by any means you choose.

- Lord, bless and empower that great company of intercessors joining this prayer battle.

- And Lord, empower all those "Joshua workers" through whom you are working out your war and judgment against all those who have made war against your people.

Praying God's Blessing on All Those Who Bless Israel and the Jewish People

While we must expose and overcome the curse of genocide as we have done, our role as intercessors is also to announce God's blessing upon all who bless Israel and the Jewish people. The theme running through all these pages is God's promise to Abraham:

> "My desire is to bless those who bless you, but whoever curses you I will curse, and in you all the families of the earth will be blessed." (Genesis 12:3 TLV)

We have spent enough time naming and breaking the curses; we must conclude with a blessing! God has revealed His heart to us: it is to pour out blessing upon those who bless the seed of Abraham and those engrafted in him through faith in Yeshua Ha Mashiach (Jesus the Messiah). God's blessing is expressed through the story of the entire Bible, but two passages describe the amazing scope of God's blessing, which is rooted in His covenant with the Jewish people.

> "Again Adonai spoke to Moses saying, "Speak to Aaron and to his sons saying: Thus you are to bless Bnei-Yisrael, by saying to them: 'Adonai bless you and keep you! Adonai make His face to shine on you and be gracious to you! Adonai turn His face toward you and grant you shalom!' In this way they are to place My Name over Bnei-Yisrael, and so I will bless them." (Numbers 6:22-27 TLV)

This "shalom," or peace, is multidimensional, meaning abundant life, peace, liberty, and prosperity. It will mean biblical justice and equality in our own lives and also in our families, communities, and nations. These are wonderful temporal, common grace blessings that have been visited upon the Jewish people and those who bless them. We pray these blessings upon those who are living under the curse of having cursed the Jews. Right now, we especially pray this blessing upon the people of Gaza and all others who are under the demonic and political bondage of Islamists who are breathing death curses against the Jews.

All this is good, but the ultimate blessing and Shalom flow from being born again into God's everlasting kingdom through Yeshua the Messiah:

> "No one has gone up into heaven except the One who came down from heaven—the Son of Man. Just as Moses lifted up the serpent in the desert, so the Son of Man must be lifted up, so that whoever believes in Him may have eternal life! "For God so loved the world

that He gave His one and only Son, that whoever believes in Him shall not perish but have eternal life. God did not send the Son into the world to condemn the world, but in order that the world might be saved through Him." (John 3:13-17 TLV)

This is what we pray earnestly for all those involved in God's war with our generation's manifestation of Amalek. We believe that what Satan intended for evil, God is going to use for great good. Praying for that to happen through this great revival brings us to our concluding chapter.

11

As One New Humanity, Preparing for a Great Outpouring of the Holy Spirit

In this final chapter, let's return to this motif that has governed our discernment, prayer work, and prophetic declarations: the battle with the Amalekites recorded in Exodus 17. The battle had to be fought because the Amalekites, who did not fear God, had chosen the path of death, attacking the Israelites at their time of significant vulnerability in order to prevent them from keeping their rendezvous with God at Mt. Sinai. This was to be the decisive meeting with God in which He was to make the covenant with them that formed them into "a kingdom of priests and a holy nation" (Exodus 19:4-6). Suppose the battle had been lost and the Amalekites had succeeded in killing Moses and Joshua and scattering the motley band who were coming out of Egypt. In that case, God's salvation plans for humanity would have been aborted, which was no doubt Satan's intention. Of course, the Lord God was aware of this, so He directed Moses in a unique battle strategy that could defeat both the human and demonic forces.

Chapter 11 As One New Humanity Preparing for a Great Outpouring of the Holy Spirit

Then God announced that He would have war with Amalek for all generations, and that He would utterly blot out the memory of the Amalekites from under heaven (Exodus 17:14). Take note that this war that God declares, with its goal of wiping out a people, is not a war declared against everyone and every movement that threatens the fulfillment of God's redemptive plans through the Jewish people and those engrafted into them. If this had been the case, then God's wrath and judgment would have consumed us all. God's declaration of war to wipe out His enemies is against those who have chosen the means of genocide against His people, seeking to prevent them from being the embodiment of His Kingdom and a means of blessing on earth. In the biblical account this included Haman in the book of Esther, in the 1930s and 1940s it was the Nazis, and now it is Hamas and all the others who have chosen the goal of exterminating the Jews.

In this short book we have discussed how God calls us to join in this war against the present-day Amalekites – those people who have no fear of God and who, in their words and deeds, have joined in with Satan's plans of extermination, starting with Jews. Joining in God's war against them has been an urgent necessity of this season. However, this is not our complete calling, and neither is it the focus of our specific ministry, Presbyterian Reformed Ministries International.

Our focus is praying to advance the Kingdom of God into all the earth - to all peoples and nations. Our particular role in this great missionary task is taking part with the Triune God in preparing for, and igniting, outpourings of the Holy Spirit for advancing the Gospel of the Kingdom to all nations and restoring the Kingdom to Israel through Jesus Christ. This is where our heart and passion are; our commitment is to this overarching kingdom goal.

However, this call to join God's war against the present embodiment of Amalek – Hamas and those dedicated to the destruction of Israel and the extermination of the Jewish people – is an unfortunate but urgent necessity. While it may seem like a diversion from our primary calling of fulfilling the Gospel mission that God has given us, in fact it is essential and intrinsic to our mission to advance the Kingdom by preparing for and igniting waves of the Holy Spirit. The reason is that at this time in history, unlike all other periods of revival history, all the conditions for a move of the Holy Spirit to fulfill the conditions for Christ's return in glory are present.

Chief among these in our present epoch is the fulfillment of biblical prophecy concerning the Jewish people and the Gospel of the Kingdom being preached to all nations. Jews have returned to the Land of Israel. There is the messianic movement in which Jews are coming to faith in Yeshua the Messiah while retaining their Jewishness. There is growing unity between born-again Jews and Gentiles as the "One New Man," being baptized together with the Holy Spirit as empowered witnesses to Yeshua the Messiah. This is portrayed in the chart below:

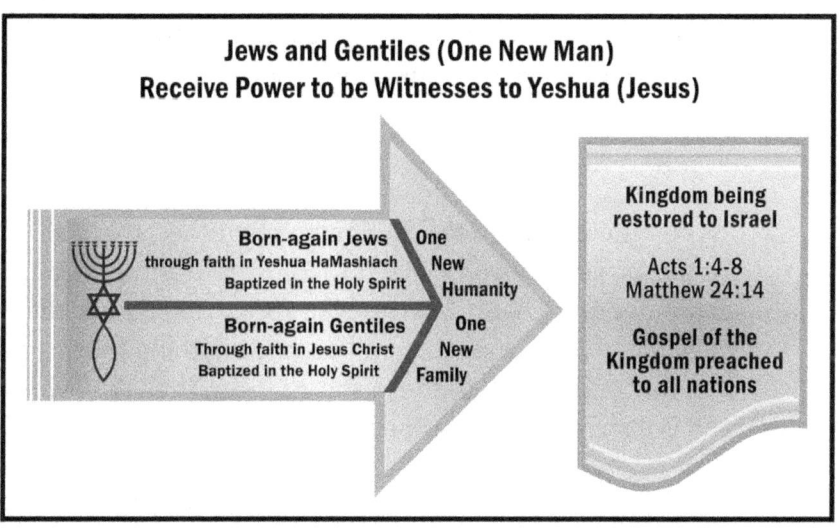

In PRMI, we are seeing this amazing unity taking place, healing the most fundamental breach within the body of Christ between born-again Jews and Gentiles. We are experiencing Jesus (Yeshua) forgiving us of present and generational wounding, healing His body! He is overcoming Jew-hatred with love, and born-again Jews

Chapter 11 As One New Humanity Preparing for a Great Outpouring of the Holy Spirit

are overcoming antagonism to the cross with gratitude that it was the means of salvation for us all. We are actively working in partnerships together. Indeed, this book has been written with the help of firsthand experience of Messianic Jews and born-again Gentiles taking part together in strategic-level intercession and spiritual warfare. This partnership started long before the October 7th Hamas Massacre of the Jews but has only deepened and will continue to grow because this partnership is essential in God's plans to defeat these curses of genocide and ignite global revival.

Added to this role of the One New Humanity are the other elements crucial for the great outpouring of the Holy Spirit. We are experiencing the fulfillment of Smith Wigglesworth's 1947 prophecy:

> "When the new church phase is on the wane, there will be evidence in the churches of something that has not been seen before: a coming together of those with an emphasis on the Word and those with an emphasis on the Spirit.
>
> "When the word and the Spirit come together, there will be the biggest move of the Holy Spirit that the nations, and indeed, the world, have ever seen. It will mark the beginning of a revival that will eclipse anything that has been witnessed within these shores, even the Wesleyan and Welsh revivals of former years."[59]

We are experiencing this within this stream of the Holy Spirit embodied in Presbyterian-Reformed Ministries international! Those with a focus on the word of God are the evangelicals in the

---

[59] https://prophecytoday.uk/study/prophetic-insights/item/389-testing-prophecies-together-smith-wigglesworth-s-1947-prophecy.html

Presbyterian and Reformed Streams, and those with a focus on the Spirit are those in the Charismatic and Pentecostal streams. In this ministry of PRMI, both of these are being fused together and the result is that we are already experiencing outpouring of the Holy Spirit in many locations and are seeing congregations on fire with the Holy Spirit and rooted in the Word of God. This integration of word and Spirit is taking place within other movements and in some denominations as well. So, praise God!

The other major indication that we are on the edge of the great revival is the unity that Jesus prayed for John 17. We are experiencing this within our particular stream of the Holy Spirit and see that it is taking place in others as well. The divisions of denominations, races and nations within the Church, are being overcome by the power of the Holy Spirit and the centrality of Jesus. We are genuinely experiencing this unity that Jesus prayed for us to have. We are not yet perfect, but we are truly seeing significant progress in fulfilling these prophecies with these manifestations of the Kingdom of God.

The result of all this coming together within the ministry of PRMI is that we are experiencing extraordinary outpourings of the Holy Spirit, with the manifest presence of Jesus Christ at all of our events and gatherings.

But PRMI is just one small stream of the Holy Spirit's flow. If we are experiencing all this in our ministry, how much more is happening in the entire global body of Christ (Messiah)? There is a vast river of God's Kingdom, with countless tributaries all surging forward in our era to bring us to the completion of the Gospel of the Kingdom being preached to all nations and the Kingdom being restored to Israel.

In past revivals and great awakenings, the part that has mostly been missing is the Jewish link and the unity of the "One New Humanity." This is the weaker, most vulnerable link in this current incredible outpouring. The reason for this is that Israel is surrounded by those who have committed themselves to her destruction and to the extermination of the Jewish people worldwide. Further, the fallen human heart is a fertile field for

Chapter 11 As One New Humanity Preparing for a Great Outpouring of the Holy Spirit

stirring up the smoldering embers of Jew-hatred. Frankly, though it is horrible to put it so bluntly, it is much easier to exterminate the 15 million or so Jews on earth than the more than 2 billion Christians.[60]

Satan has launched his attack on October 7th, 2023. At the same time, Holy Spirit revival fires are gaining great momentum, and I believe they are coming close to the tipping point and becoming the Great End Times Awakening.

My urgent prayer and hope in getting this book out to a broad audience, as well as continuing to do the work of strategic-level intercession, is this: that Satan's plans for the destruction of Israel and extermination of the Jews (and even a third World War, which would kill billions) will be thwarted and that we will soon be celebrating a great global awakening and the return of the King of Kings!

---

[60] Added to Satan's terrible calculations, if he wanted to exterminate the Jewish people, it would only take a few well-placed nuclear weapons to accomplish this terrible deed. There are 7.5 million Jews living in Israel. And 6.3 million in the United States with a larger concentration of over a million in New York City area alone. https://en.wikipedia.org/wiki/Jewish_population_by_country Given these demographic facts, the leaders of America would be foolish to ignore those who chant "Death to Israel" and "Death to America" and who are seeking the means to accomplish it.

Postscript: Engaging High-Level Demonic Powers

There is one last area that we are called into, but which must only be done at the explicit direction of the Holy Spirit. It is, in the name of Jesus Christ, breaking the power of the high-level demons behind the individuals, movements, organizations, and nations through whom Satan is carrying out his plans for the destruction of Israel and the extermination of the Jewish people.

Moving into this area of strategic level intercession and spiritual warfare must be done in well-equipped cohorts of intercessors and spiritual warriors. Equipping for this dimension is beyond the scope of this book.

I am sorry that this book must stop short of moving into this strategic level of intercession and into the detailed tactics for engaging the high-level demons. By implementing the prayer directions that we have outlined, we have already broached into this area. By exposing the deep plans of Satan for destroying Israel and the Jewish people and identifying the people and movements who are the present-day Amalekites, we have already begun to move into this sphere of strategic level intercession and spiritual warfare, engaging with high-level demons. However, Jesus Christ, the Commander of the Lord's armies, has not called us to go any further in this book into the tactics and strategies of directly engaging the high-level demons that we know are behind these evils.

Here, we are to stick to what Paul described as being prepared and taking a defensive posture rather than moving on to the offensive.

Postscript: Engaging High-level Demonic Powers

> (10) Finally, be strengthened in the Lord and in the strength of his power. (11) Clothe yourselves with the full armor of God, so that you will be able to stand against the schemes of the devil. (12) For our struggle is not against flesh and blood, but against the rulers, against the powers, against the world rulers of this darkness, against the spiritual forces of evil in the heavens.
>
> (13) For this reason, take up the full armor of God so that you may be able to stand your ground on the evil day, and having done everything, to stand. (14) Stand firm therefore, by fastening the belt of truth around your waist, by putting on the breastplate of righteousness, (15) by fitting your feet with the preparation that comes from the good news of peace, (16) and in all of this, by taking up the shield of faith with which you can extinguish all the flaming arrows of the evil one. (17) And take the helmet of salvation and the sword of the Spirit (which is the word of God). (18) With every prayer and petition, pray at all times in the Spirit, and to this end be alert, with all perseverance and petitions for all the saints. (Eph 6:10-18 NET)

We recommend that if the Holy Spirit is calling you into this dimension of strategic level intercession and spiritual warfare that you seek out further equipping in this area. We strongly counsel you that it is not wise to engage in this level of intercession on your own, so it is crucial to be a part of a fellowship that is called and equipped to do this work.

I confidently recommend the equipping that we offer in PRMI as being a good way to join God's army of intercessors. So check out our equipping programs at www.prmi.org, or join our special set-apart blog page for those called to this work: www.discernwith.us. This is called Discerning the Times, and aims to equip and provide resources for intercessors to cooperate with the Holy Spirit in advancing the kingdom of God.

Appendix C: Resources to Grow in Intercession and Spiritual Warfare

Presbyterian-Reformed Ministries International

PRMI was founded in 1966 to pray and work for the spiritual renewal of Presbyterian and Reformed churches. Over the past 50 years, we have grown to include parts of the Body of Christ in many nations and continue to have a distinctive role in the worldwide movement of the Holy Spirit advancing the Gospel of Jesus Christ for the fulfillment of the Great Commission.

www.prmi.org

Presbyterian-Reformed Ministries International offers the following opportunities to grow in the work of intercessory prayer and spiritual warfare illustrated in this book. We also provide a way for intercessors to connect into networks to participate in various prayer initiatives.

Discerning the Times

Receive **Discerning The Times**, an email digest of blogs written by Dr. Zeb Bradford Long offering discernment on current events and educating people to issues that face the Church today to mobilize intercessors.

www.discernwith.us

Other books available for mobilizing prayer for Revival

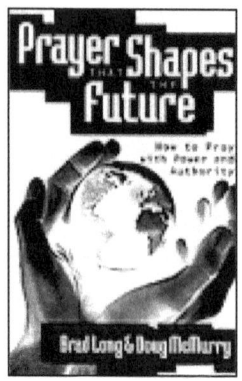

"But you will receive power when the Holy Spirit has come upon you, and you will be my witnesses in Jerusalem, and in all Judea and Samaria, and to the farthest parts of the earth."
Acts 1:8

Learn how to cooperate with the Holy Spirit to be a witness to Jesus Christ by effectively engaging in ministries of prayer, healing, spiritual warfare, and evangelism for growing the Church and advancing the Kingdom of God.

Dunamis can help you deepen your walk with the Lord and prepare you for effective ministry wherever the Lord has called you. "Dunamis" is the Greek term for "power."

With the Dunamis teaching, you'll discover:

- **Solid biblical theology about the person and work of the Holy Spirit in the life of the believer.**
- **Teaching forged from the Scriptures, proven in ministry and informed by 200 years of renewal and revival movements.**
- **Your spiritual gifts and how to use them effectively in the Kingdom of God.**
- **How to recognize God's guidance for ministry in a given moment through the experience-based lab times and review debriefings.**

The Dunamis Project consists of six units, each taught over five days and six months apart in the same location. Each event consists of intensive biblical teaching and practical application in prayer and worship. These events are designed to enable every believer to grow in their faith and personal relationship with God and participate in the ministry of the Holy Spirit. For more information, go to www.prmi.org.

www.ingramcontent.com/pod-product-compliance
Lightning Source LLC
LaVergne TN
LVHW051101080426
835508LV00019B/2000